THE BONES OF TOMORROW

What Time Teaches On Meaning, Belonging, and the Gift of Years

Renae C. Linde

CRF Luttrell

© 2025 by Cynthia RF Luttrell

All rights reserved...

ISBN: 979-8-9930830-0-1

No portion of this book may be reproduced, stored, or transmitted in any form or by any means, electronic, mechanical, photocopying, recording, or otherwise, without the prior written permission from the copyright owner, except in the case of brief quotations embodied in reviews or articles as permitted by U.S. copyright law.

An Independent Publication by CRF Luttrell

For Jennifer, Rod, Kenny Ray, and Miss Emma

*You shaped me without trying to.
With steadiness, truth, radiance, and presence,
you showed me how to live with integrity.
This book carries your echo.*

And for Ryla,
You shape me still.

CONTENTS

A Phone Call with My Dad — 1

ACT I: Becoming — 5

1. Learning to Be — 7
2. Young and Trying — 23
3. Becoming Real — 35

ACT II: Belonging — 49

4. The Work of Love — 51
5. Career and Calling — 65
6. When the Mirror Shifts — 83
7. Becoming an Elder-in-Training — 93

Act III: Blessing — 103

8. The Gift of Redirection — 105
9. Letting Light Spill — 115
10. The Fullness of Time — 129

None of It Was Wasted — 143

References

A PHONE CALL WITH MY DAD

We didn't talk for long, maybe twenty minutes. One of our usual check-ins, the kind that had become more common as the years gathered behind us.

That evening's subject was time, how it accelerates, folds in on itself, slips loose from the usual rules. He was past eighty. Still traveling, still quick in mind, but I could hear in his voice what his words didn't name: the slower pace between sentences, the softened edges of his tone. His questions still cut to the heart, his listening still deliberate, but the current underneath had shifted.

I was on speaker, moving through my evening, feeding the dogs, stacking papers, catching the hiss of onions in the skillet between sentences.

"I think life has three acts," I told him. "The first, learning to become an adult. The middle, living as one. The last, offering what you've gathered."

He gave a quiet laugh. Not dismissing it, more as if the neatness surprised him. Still, he stayed with the thought, asked me to keep going.

In my mind, the acts carried names: Becoming, Belonging, Blessing.

I hadn't said them out loud, but that was the shape I remembered later. Something inside me settled into place.

We weren't trading theology or quoting philosophers. We were speaking from the slow schooling of years, wisdom shaped by ache and by looking back. I'd heard many frameworks before, but this wasn't one. It felt more like a mirror.

I saw then how I'd already been living the sequence. The first act, Becoming, had been full of striving, wanting to be good, loved, worthy. I chased approval, collected tools and stories, wore identities that fit for a season.

The second act, Belonging, turned me inward toward application: work, family, faith. Offering what I carried while still learning what it was. Asking less "Who am I?" and more "What is mine to give?" It was grounding, investing, recalibrating. Holy.

Now, as I write, I stand in the third act, Blessing. The pace has changed. Fewer masks. Different measures. A readiness to pour out what I have, even if it looks quieter than before. It's not about scarcity. It's about living from a place already made whole.

That conversation gave me language, and with it, permission.

The world I knew measured worth by proof, progress, relevance, impact. But the soul doesn't move by those coordinates. It circles. It spirals. It returns to familiar questions with changed eyes. It seeks integration over performance.

What my dad and I touched that night was a rhythm deeper than achievement, a way of living that expands instead of peaks.

That phone call didn't reroute my life, but it named something I already sensed: the old maps no longer worked. Time felt less like a ladder and more like a tide. I wasn't reaching for the next rung. I was listening. Watching. Returning.

This book lives inside that rhythm.

It's shaped by faith, not formula, rooted in Scripture and the life of Christ, drawn from the deep well of biblical wisdom. It's shaped by the patterns of mind and body, by research in development and healing that reminds us we keep becoming, even in the later decades. It's shaped by philosophy's long reach toward meaning, and by story, because truth rarely reaches us in theory; it arrives in the lived moments where someone else says, "Me too."

If you're in transition, if your questions have outgrown your answers, if time feels altered, if you long for more than momentum, you're not alone. You may be between identities, done striving but unsure what to do with your strength. Your body may be shifting, your rhythms resetting, and you may be asking what this next season requires of you.

This book is written for that wondering. It's a companion, not a prescription.

Each chapter follows one movement of the sequence through story, Scripture, science, and memory. Together, they invite you to measure life less by output and more by presence, attention, meaning.

That conversation with my dad, ordinary, unadorned, became a threshold. It reminded me that wisdom doesn't always arrive in grand moments. Sometimes it slips through the line of a phone call and stays with you.

Three acts. One life. A rhythm worth keeping.

Becoming. Belonging. Blessing.

And all of it sacred.

ACT 1: BECOMING

The Act of Learning

Chapter One
Learning to Be

First Mirrors: Who Told Me Who I Was?

Before I ever asked who I was, I had already been told. Not with poetry. Not with tenderness. But with tone, with silence, with the sharpness of a parent's gaze when you get it wrong, and the occasional softness when you get it "right."

The truth is, I didn't grow up with mirrors. I grew up with spotlights and shadows. Mirrors are neutral. They reflect what's there. A spotlight tells you where to stand, and a shadow tells you where not to be. That was the rhythm of our house. The performance, the punishment, the guessing game of how to be good enough today.

In early childhood, we don't develop identity in isolation. We borrow it. We borrow it from the faces around us, from how we're treated, from the labels we're handed before we can speak for ourselves. If someone calls you "smart," you learn to answer to it. If someone calls you "difficult," you carry it like a scar. And if you're told nothing at all, if your presence is met with indifference or volatility, you learn to study the air for cues. You shape-shift. You learn fast. Faster than you should have to.

In our house, you didn't meet your reflection. You read the temperature. You read tone. My mother's tenderness had a short shelf life. Her fury didn't. It could fill a room in an instant. My stepfather hovered in the background, physically present but emotionally off duty. And so my sister and I began to pattern ourselves, staying alert, recalibrating as needed, passing the role of "good child" back and forth depending on what set her off. Sometimes we were both the target. Sometimes, in rare moments, we were both spared.

You don't realize it at the time, but you're learning something essential. You're learning what love feels like. And more dangerously, you're learning what you have to become in order to feel loved.

It took me decades to untangle the versions of myself I had built in response to other people's projections. Longer still to believe that God had anything different to say about who I was.

I wish I could say I went straight from survival to freedom. I didn't. I didn't find freedom right away. I just changed stages. Left one performance behind and picked up a new one. At home, I'd trained myself to anticipate moods. Out in the world, I refined that same instinct, called it charisma, competence, likability. I learned what each setting wanted and adjusted accordingly. I made myself agreeable, impressive, efficient. People called me strong. They thought they were complimenting me. Maybe they were. But what they saw as composure was really calibration. I wasn't showing up strong, I was showing up prepared. Always alert. Always adjusting. Trying to stay just far enough out of view to avoid becoming a target.

That kind of strength doesn't come from the soul. It comes from necessity. It isn't rooted. It reacts.

The first time I read Genesis with clear eyes, I saw something I hadn't been taught to see: that before God asked anything of Adam and Eve, He blessed them. Before they performed, before they proved, before they even understood what they were, He called them good.

"So God created mankind in his own image, in the image of God he created them; male and female he created them. God blessed them..." (Genesis 1:27–28a, NIV)

Blessed. Before performance. Before obedience. Before error.

That's the original mirror: a God who sees you and says, you are mine. A God who doesn't flinch at your becoming, who doesn't need you to be fixed before He calls you beloved. That was not the mirror I grew up with. But it is the mirror I now return to.

Developmental psychology calls it reflected appraisal, the process by which we form a sense of self based on how others respond to us. In early life, the child's sense of identity isn't shaped by internal conviction, but by external cues: "You're helpful." "You're in the way." "You're always making things harder." Those words stick. Not just in memory, but in the nervous system.

By the time we reach adolescence, we've usually compiled a mental archive of who we are, based on feedback from parents, peers, teachers, sometimes God, though often filtered through the behaviors of those who claimed to speak for Him.

Research supports this, especially attachment theory. Children raised in unpredictable or unsafe environments often develop either an anxious or avoidant attachment style, constantly scanning for threats or suppressing their needs to avoid rejection (Bowlby, 1988). I didn't know those terms at the time. But I knew the posture: brace, monitor, adjust. Become what keeps the peace. Stay out of the blast radius.

And over time, the mirror gets warped. You stop asking who you are. You start asking what will make you acceptable.

There's a philosophical concept known as coherence theory, the idea that truth is what fits into a consistent web of belief. But in fragmented families, the "web" never forms cleanly. There's no central truth to build around. Only emotional reactions and unspoken rules. What's good today might be punishable tomorrow. What gets praised in public gets punished behind closed doors. There's no logic to it, only compliance.

And so you build a self that fits. Even if it isn't true. Even if it's quietly killing you.

That's the ache of incoherence. You're not exactly living a lie, but you really don't know what the truth is anymore. You've been handed so many definitions of who you are, most of them wrong, some of them harmful, and your soul has become crowded with contradictions.

Who told me who I was?

A rigid mother. A quiet father. A television family I wanted to believe in. A God who seemed like He might be watching, but never interrupted the storm.

That's who.

Until the day came when I started asking a new question: What if they were all wrong?

What if my soul remembered something they had forgotten?

What if the truest thing about me is the one thing they never said, that I was already loved?

Foundations and Fractures: Belief Systems in Childhood

Children believe what they're told, but more than that, they believe what they see. And what I saw, growing up, was that power didn't have to explain itself. That fear kept people in line more effectively than love. That God was someone who watched from the corners, nodding when punishment was delivered and turning away when it went too far.

That wasn't theology. That was household logic.

We went to church every Sunday. Lutheran pews, folded bulletins, adult sermons delivered to children without translation. I didn't mind it, there was something orderly about it, something that stayed in place. But the God we heard about from the pulpit felt unrelated to the one I was being taught at home.

My mother believed in a wrathful God. Not in name, she never said that outright. But in tone, in volume, in what she allowed and punished. She used Scripture like a belt. You didn't question it. You didn't interpret it. You obeyed. And if you didn't, you weren't just disobedient. You were wicked. Rebellious. Spiritually defective.

I never saw her read the Bible cover to cover, but she knew the verses that gave her control. *"Children, obey your parents in the Lord." "Spare the rod." "Honor thy mother."* That one got repeated often. It wasn't for comfort. She used it to reinforce control, firm, unquestioned, final.

So belief didn't grow from mystery or awe. It formed under pressure. I learned early that God was watching, and that His version of patience looked too familiar, thin, unstable, earned. If you followed the rules, you might stay in good standing. If not, the consequences came quickly, and they came hard. Not just from heaven, but from the kitchen, the hallway, the car.

That was the shape of my early theology: a spiritualized survival system.

There was no language in our house for grace.

No wonder. Grace isn't transactional. And everything in our home was. Love was earned. Peace was a reward for good behavior. Tenderness was fleeting and usually followed by some form of correction. You didn't rest in love. You earned it, if you were lucky. You kept it, if you were careful.

Even joy felt conditional.

It's a strange thing, growing up with a God you fear more than trust. You internalize the rules, but not the relationship. You learn the choreography of repentance, apologize quickly, promise to do better, but you don't actually believe you're safe. You believe you're being monitored. Evaluated.

For a long time, I didn't pray unless I was in trouble. And even then, I wasn't sure if I was allowed to ask for anything. I assumed God, like my mother, had a ledger. And that mine wasn't looking good.

But even in that tight, rule-bound faith, something else stirred.

I remember reading about David. Not the sanitized flannel-graph version, but the story itself, raw, surprising, full of action. I was a kid, so what struck me wasn't his failures. It was the slingshot. The fact that he stepped onto a battlefield with nothing but a stone and a strange kind of confidence. No armor. No fear. Just faith.

That part got inside me. I didn't understand his flaws, or what it meant to be a man after God's own heart. I didn't even think of him as complicated. He was a kid, like me. I just knew he trusted God, and God seemed to trust him right back. That stuck. Not because I understood it, but because it felt... different. Braver. Closer.

I wouldn't have had language for it then. But looking back, I can see it left a mark. Not a switch-flip. Just a small place inside me that stayed open. A story I'd come back to later, when I needed to believe that God could use someone unpolished. Someone still in the process of becoming.

In psychology, they call it relational mapping, the way children come to know God through the people who claim to represent Him. A child's theology isn't built from doctrine. It's built from experience. Safety, or lack of it. Warmth, or withdrawal. Who you believe God is will always be shaped first by who made you feel seen, or didn't. If caregivers are warm and responsive, God is often imagined as nurturing. If caregivers are cold, volatile, or abusive, God is often seen as distant, punitive, or inconsistent (Rizzuto, 1979; Granqvist, 2002).

And once those early templates are set, they're not easily dislodged. Even as adults, we tend to filter spiritual experiences through the relational blueprints we learned young. It takes real work, psychological and spiritual, to uncouple God from the human figures who first introduced Him.

This is why so many people deconstruct later in life. It's not that they lost faith, but their faith was fused to systems of harm or control. To disentangle that is not rebellion. It's restoration.

In my case, the God of my early years was too fused with fear to feel like freedom. But that wasn't because God wasn't there. It was because the way I was taught had more to do with control than with Christ.

And yet, I clung to faith, even when I didn't know what to do with it. Because something in me believed there had to be more. A deeper source. A truer presence.

I didn't know, then, that I was longing for the real God.

The one who never needed me to be small in order to be holy.

It would be easy to write off those early belief systems as useless. Harmful. Worth discarding. And in some ways, they were. They taught me to mistrust joy. To suppress my instincts. To spiritualize dysfunction. That damage ran deep.

But they also gave me a kind of scaffolding. Imperfect, but present. A rhythm of sacred things. A knowing that there was more than the visible world. A hunger for the divine, even if it was dressed in fear. My mother's theology was rule-bound, shaped by duty and reverence, heavy on the "Thou shalt not." She emphasized obedience, the Ten Commandments, the authority of parents. And yet, within that structure, something steady was passed down. She named God for me. She gave me Jesus as a character in the story. We prayed before meals and at bedtime, and those prayers became a rhythm I shared with my own child. I didn't understand God then. I didn't long for Him. But the scaffolding was there. And some part of it held.

It took years to realize what needed to be kept and what needed to be undone. I had to rebuild the language. The tone. The image of God I'd grown up with. But I wasn't starting from nothing, I was starting from memory. From a name I'd heard in childhood, and wondered about. From practices that had formed muscle memory, even if my heart wasn't yet involved.

Eventually, something deeper did begin to stir. A quiet ache for the God behind the rules. A hope, thin at first, that He might be different from how I was first introduced.

And He was.

"You shall know the truth, and the truth shall make you free." (John 8:32, KJV)

The truth wasn't just that God existed. The truth was that He loved me, and always had.

That He didn't need my performance.

That He wasn't waiting to punish me.

That He was already near, even when I couldn't feel it.

My early belief system cracked under pressure, but through the break, something deeper emerged. Presence replaced performance. Relationship became the center. Rest took the place of striving.

This is the ground I live on now, formed slowly, intentionally, in rhythm with a God who kept His gaze steady. He saw me through all the turning, all the hiding, all the years I couldn't see myself.

Identity and Image: Made in God's Image, Shaped by Environment

When you grow up inside distortion, it takes a long time to trust that what you feel is real.

The body knows it first. The gut tightens. The shoulders curl in. The breath becomes shallow. But the mind, conditioned to dismiss and explain, takes longer to catch up. Especially when the distortion comes wrapped in the language of love. Especially when the people around you act like it's normal.

This is the paradox of early identity: we are made in the image of God, yet shaped by environments that rarely reflect Him. And so we learn to perform the versions of ourselves that keep us safest. We adapt. We shrink. We disown parts of our being just to stay within the lines we were told were holy.

But image and environment are not the same. And one, thank God, runs deeper than the other.

"So God created mankind in his own image, in the image of God he created them..." (Genesis 1:27, NIV)

Not in the image of fear. Not in the image of scarcity. Not even in the image of the people who misused His name.

In His image.

That means something. It has to.

Even when I couldn't feel it, even when I had no language for it, something in me knew I had been made for more than compliance. That the part of me that longed for justice, for truth, for steadiness, for peace, that part wasn't rebellion. It was reflection. Of Him.

But that's not what I was told.

I was told I was too intense. Too stubborn. Rebellious. I learned to file those things under "flaws." I tried to become agreeable, neutral, pleasing. I turned my volume down so low I could barely hear myself. That's how early environments shape us. They don't mold us into something true, they train us to mute what already was.

The image of God wasn't something I had to earn. It was something I had to unearth.

Psychologists use the term false self to describe the persona a child develops in response to emotionally unsafe environments. It's strategy. The false self is built out of necessity: if I show you who I really am, and you reject it, I won't survive. So instead, I show you what you seem to want. I give you a version of me you can manage. And over time, I forget it's not the whole story.

Winnicott, who coined the term, emphasized that this isn't a disorder. It's protection. A necessary adaptation when the true self isn't welcomed.

But the tragedy is this: if no one ever reflects our real self back to us, we stop believing it exists.

That's what happened to me over time. Piece by piece, I internalized that the parts of me that felt most alive were the parts that got me into trouble. My questions. My convictions. My drive. My tenderness. The image of God was there, bright and aching, but I learned to bury it.

I don't think I'm alone in that.

So many of us reach adulthood not knowing who we are, only who we learned to be. We don't know how to separate personality from self-protection. We've spent so long trying to be manageable that when someone asks us what we want, we flinch.

And yet. God's image remains. Underneath it all.

Unruined. Unrevoked.

No amount of shaping can erase the imprint of God's breath.

If I had only known God as Creator, I think I might have stayed lost in the idea of Him. But Jesus, God incarnate, changed the equation. He didn't just tell people who they were. He showed them. He called out image in places where everyone else saw shame.

The woman at the well. The tax collector in the tree. The leper who no one would touch. These were stories of compassion, and they were stories of restoration. Jesus didn't wait for people to prove themselves before He spoke identity over them.

He saw them. Then He told them the truth.

That was revolutionary to me. Because everything in my early shaping said, "Be clean first. Be right first. Be better first."

But Jesus says:

"You are the light of the world…" (Matthew 5:14, NIV)

Not you will be. You are.

That's identity.

Not an achievement.

A declaration.

And I needed that. I needed to know that the parts of me that had been called too much or too wrong were actually evidence of design. That my longing for justice wasn't defiance, it was divine DNA. That my hunger for truth wasn't rebellion, it was remembering.

I needed to know I hadn't lost the image. I'd just been taught to doubt it.

The shaping of our early years is powerful. But it's not sovereign. It can mar us. Distort us. Even traumatize us. But it cannot undo the core of who we are in Christ.

That's what I didn't understand for years. I thought healing would mean going back, finding the original wound, fixing the pattern. But healing, for me, didn't look like repair. It looked like revelation.

Not everything that formed me gets to define me.

Some of it can stay. Some of it must go.

That's what this movement of Becoming is. It's uncovering the self that already exists, intact, beloved, and waiting to be recognized. The self God already saw. Already loved. Already called.

And even now, I'm still learning to believe Him.

I'm still learning to believe that I bear His image, not because of what I've done, but because of what He decided.

Curiosity and Conscience: Early Awareness of Right, Wrong, and Mystery

Some of my earliest questions weren't about fairness, they were about mercy.

Not in those words, of course. I wouldn't have known to call it that. But I remember wondering why some kids got second chances and others didn't. I saw it early. Some adults exploded and walked away clean. Others, kids like my sister and me, got punished for the smallest look, the wrong tone, the truth said too plainly. The rules shifted. The goalposts moved. What passed for discipline usually looked more like control.

At some point, I stopped asking what would get me in trouble and started asking what actually felt right. That's when I knew I had something deeper than fear, something like a moral core, even if I didn't have words for it yet. I didn't always follow it. But I heard it. And I didn't understand how the people in charge didn't seem to hear it too.

What I didn't know then, but know now, is that children begin developing moral awareness far earlier than most adults assume. Developmental theorist Lawrence Kohlberg described early moral reasoning as reward-and-punishment driven, basic, survival-focused. But even inside that, something more begins to take shape. A gut sense that certain choices carry weight. That some actions feel connected to something larger, even if no one explains why.

In rigid spiritual homes, that kind of intuition can feel suspect. That voice inside, the one that says this isn't right, gets ignored first.

I kept my questions to myself.

They didn't come from books or sermons. They rose up on their own, uninvited. I never asked them out loud, I wouldn't have known where to place them. But they lived in me anyway.

How can God hear everyone at once?

What happens to babies who die?

Why do we sit still in church if Jesus wants us to rejoice?

Why did Pharaoh keep saying no?

There had to be more than what I was being told. More to God. More to life. More to the rules that didn't sit quite right in my body. I just couldn't shake the sense that something was missing. That faith, if it was real, had to be deeper than fear and broader than obedience.

I didn't want escape. I wanted reality. Something solid. Something spacious enough to hold the questions I hadn't yet learned to speak aloud.

That instinct, to question, to press, to wonder, was treated with suspicion in the environment I was raised in. But biblically, it's woven into the very fabric of faith.

Abraham questioned.

Moses doubted.

Job raged.

Mary pondered.

Even Jesus, in His twelve-year-old body, stayed behind in the temple to ask questions no one else was asking (Luke 2:46).

That isn't disobedience. That's sacred curiosity.

And in a house where obedience was everything, curiosity became my private form of resistance. I didn't fight. I observed. I didn't argue. I reflected. I stored things up and let them ferment.

Some of those questions broke open later in life. Some still haven't found an answer. But they've all drawn me closer to the God I now know, the One who isn't threatened by wonder, who is wonder.

It's a dangerous thing when morality is reduced to compliance.

I remember being punished for telling the truth. Not because I'd done something wrong, but because the truth embarrassed someone. I picked it up early: telling the truth could cost you. Especially when power didn't want to be challenged.

So I adjusted. Took things out. Chose different words. Kept the edges dull.

Even then, something inside kept noticing. Rules that shifted to suit the moment. Punishment dressed up as principle. A gap between what was said and what was lived.

Eventually, a question settled in and stayed there, low and unresolved.

If this was supposed to be holy, why did it feel like control?

I wouldn't have used the word integrity back then. But that's what I was trying to preserve. Some sense of alignment. Of goodness that wasn't about punishment or posturing, but about presence.

And slowly, God began to show me that real goodness doesn't need to dominate. It doesn't need a spotlight. It doesn't need to win.

It just needs to be true.

Scripture doesn't speak often about conscience, but when it does, it's not framed as self-reliance. It's framed as God-breathed discernment.

"The Spirit himself testifies with our spirit that we are God's children." (Romans 8:16, NIV)

That's the mystery I couldn't name as a child, the way something inside me felt different than the voices around me. Not better. Not arrogant. Just...not in agreement. And not because I was resisting faith. But because I was longing for a truer version of it.

As a child, I didn't know to call it conscience. I just knew when something didn't feel right. When the rules felt wrong. When silence felt heavy. But now I can look back and see what was already beginning, the slow shaping of discernment.

I used to think conscience was just about guilt. But over time, I've learned it's something quieter. More relational. It isn't self-made morality. It's a way of listening. A tuning-in. And when formed in relationship with God's Spirit, it becomes both a compass and a place of communion.

Some of the most sacred moments in my life haven't happened in sanctuaries. They've happened in those quiet reckonings, when I hear that whisper: This is not the way.

Or: That truth was costly, but you told it.

Or simply: You are safe to ask.

That's what I missed in childhood. Not just safety from harm, but safety to wonder. To explore. To be met, not managed.

But that's what the Spirit now gives me. And that is no small healing.

Children are often closer to God than we think. They aren't afraid to say, "I don't know."

And that's where mystery lives, in the space between what is and what might be.

My earliest spiritual memories weren't doctrinal. They were sensory. A bird's wings flickering in sunlight. A storm moving over a field. That strange, quiet certainty that someone saw me. That someone stayed. Someone cared.

That's the mystery I've returned to in adulthood, not the mystery that confuses, but the one that communes.

I think about how many of us were taught to question ourselves before we ever questioned what we were being taught about God. How many learned to override their instincts in order to stay within the lines. Where curiosity could feel like a threat. Where even the quiet nudge of conscience was treated as suspicion.

And that childhood sense of God, the one who felt close, steady, maybe even kind, got treated like make-believe.

But I don't think it was false.

I think it was the truest part.

Chapter Two

YOUNG AND TRYING

The First Taste of Freedom

My early adulthood wasn't some clean break into independence. It was messy. Back-and-forth. One foot in one state at my dad's, where the IT systems seed was planted. It was just a glimpse, but it stuck. The other foot was half the country away with my mom. I wasn't trying to "find myself", I was trying to stay housed, keep moving, and not go under.

I enrolled in technical college to study IT when I landed back with mom, but I dropped out after the first semester. I didn't have time to flounder. I needed to eat, pay rent, keep the lights on. I started waiting tables, then moved on to bartending at a nice restaurant. From there, I found work at a nightclub, cocktail waitress first, then behind the bar. Eventually I made it to a country club.

The hours were late. The money was decent. And the lifestyle? Pure survival disguised as a good time. I'd party until 6 a.m., crash until 2 p.m., then do it all over again. It wasn't sustainable, but it worked, for a while.

And through it all, I still had a thread of hope, stretched taut beneath the noise: I dreamed of breaking into IT. That dream held, even if I couldn't chase it directly. Even in the middle of the chaos, I was scanning the horizon for a way in.

Freedom, when it came, wasn't romantic. It didn't arrive with a ceremony or a key to a new apartment. It came in flickers, moments when no one was watching, no one was correcting me, no one was asking me to be anything but awake and paying my own bills. I'd come home from a shift, collapse on a sagging couch, eat cold leftovers, and realize, no one cared how I chewed, how I looked, or whether I was "respectful enough."

And it felt… strange. Not triumphant. Not sad. Just unfamiliar.

Freedom is terrifying when you've never had it.

I didn't know how to fill the space I'd fought so hard to claim. I still didn't trust my preferences. I wasn't confused, and I certainly didn't need coddling. I needed time to figure things out without someone breathing down my neck.

Psychologists call this space between external adulthood and internal ownership "developmental lag." But I wasn't lagging. I was adapting. Improvising. Building from scratch with no blueprint, no capital, and no fallback plan.

I'd left the house. But not the reflexes.

And still, somehow, I made it work.

The Book of Exodus tells the story of people delivered from bondage, only to wander the wilderness in disarray (Exodus 13–17). They were free, and still scared. Still longing for the predictability of Egypt when the desert got too quiet. I get it. When everything is unfamiliar, even captivity can start to look comfortable.

But God didn't scold them for their confusion. He didn't demand instant maturity. He walked with them, day after day. Fed them. Gave them water. Let them rage. And didn't leave.

I think that's what God was doing with me in those years. I wasn't praying, not in any formal way. But I was still reaching, through instinct, through exhaustion, through hunger for something steady. And I believe He met me there.

Culture sells us the "freedom narrative" like it's all momentum and self-discovery. But the truth is quieter. Less glamorous. Most of us aren't stumbling because we're lost, we're stumbling because no one ever gave us space to learn slowly. To ask dumb questions. To fail safely.

One night, about six months into living on my own, I dropped a pot of spaghetti. Sauce hit everything, floor, stove, cabinets. I stood there holding the lid, not moving. Just taking in the scene.

Then I let out a laugh. Small. Sharp. More like a release than anything else.

I didn't get upset or rush to clean it up. I just let it be, one ridiculous, unfiltered moment.

Somewhere in that moment, something shifted. I didn't name it then, but it felt like space. Like I had room for a different kind of life, even if I didn't know what it was yet.

Building with Broken Tools

I built my early adulthood like someone patching a roof in a windstorm.

No manual. No mentorship. Just instincts, urgency, and whatever tools I could find along the way.

The world around me made it sound like this season was about growth, career ladders, five-year plans, "becoming your best self."

What I was doing didn't look like that. I was hustling from job to job, learning how to manage bills, navigate adult relationships, and stay upright. And somehow, I kept going.

People called it a phase. It wasn't. It was a stretch of life I carried with full weight, bartending until 2 a.m., partying hard, sleeping past noon, then doing it all again. I moved fast because I had to. Every choice had a cost. But even in that chaos, I kept one part of myself facing forward: I still wanted to break into IT. That was the true line I followed. Quietly. Constantly.

Psychologists talk about developmental trauma as a disruption in early trust, where coregulation gets replaced with constant scanning. You learn to rely on yourself, even before you're equipped. You get good at reading people. At performing stability. At anticipating moods before they shift. You adapt quickly. But you pay for it later, when the pretending starts to feel like the only thing keeping you safe.

I never lost my drive. But for years, I used it to build a version of adulthood that looked right from the outside. I knew how to show up early. I took the jobs, paid the bills, played the part. And still, I carried tension like armor.

No one teaches you how to feel safe in your own life after growing up around volatility. I didn't know how to relate to people who weren't from my own familiar sphere of influence. So I guessed. I played the light-hearted, fun one. The party girl. Easy to be around, just distracting enough. It got smiles. It got invitations. But not depth. Not respect.

Most of my relationships stayed shallow. We didn't talk about where we came from. We talked about plans, shifts, whose place we were going to after the bar. That was the level. And I kept it there because anything deeper felt risky.

I see now how much effort I poured into creating something steady, at work, in friendships, in whatever space I called home. Not because I trusted any of it. But because I didn't want to keep bracing for collapse. I needed life to be steady, even if I had to build it from scratch every week.

That's what you do when you're building with broken tools. You overfunction. You keep things running by sheer will. You hold the whole thing up because letting go isn't an option.

It's easy to mistake that kind of life for maturity. From the outside, it looks competent. Inside, it's pure triage.

Psalm 127 says, *"Unless the Lord builds the house, the builders labor in vain."* I used to hear that like a threat. Now I hear the relief inside it. Because we all start with what we've got, duct tape, secondhand framing, borrowed wisdom. And God doesn't wait for us to get it right. He blesses what holds for as long as it needs to. And when it gives out, He stays with us through the rebuild.

The kind of faith I hold now doesn't ask for polish. It pays attention to the effort, what it costs to keep going, to keep building with whatever you've got left.

People like to say your twenties are for self-discovery. Maybe that's true for some. Mine were about staying employed, fixing what I could, and patching up the rest. You learn how to function with no insulation. You show up on little sleep. You keep the power on and your pride intact, even when everything feels temporary. Where you say yes to jobs you hate because they give you room to save. Where your instincts are sharp, your timing is fast, and your capacity to endure would stun most people, though they'll never know.

And still, we build.

We build with half-maps. With recycled tools. With voices in our heads still echoing the past.

And somehow, through all of it, something good begins to take shape. A coworker who becomes your closest ally. A small opportunity that opens a door. A space of your own that actually starts to feel like home.

I didn't have a linear path. But I had traction. Every job taught me something. Every stretch of chaos made me quicker on my feet. Every hard season clarified what I didn't want to carry forward.

I didn't build a picture-perfect life.

But I learned how to hold a hammer. How to repair what others ignored. How to lay the early framework for something better.

And that, without question, was enough.

When Nothing Felt Solid

There's a particular kind of loneliness that doesn't announce itself. It doesn't come with tears or isolation or empty rooms. It comes when your life is full of motion, full of noise, full of people, and none of it feels anchored.

It was during those restless years that I met the man who would become my partner. What began as possibility soon became entanglement, hope and tension braided together. I wanted family, but I also wanted control. I believed that if I could manage the environment, keep the peace, meet expectations, I could protect what I was building.

That was my life in my mid-twenties.

I was working. Paying bills. In a relationship that looked fine from the outside. I smiled in photos. I showed up to birthdays. I changed the oil, and replaced the carburetor. But underneath all that function was a growing tremor, a quiet panic that I had no real center.

The routines were there. The scaffolding was intact. But nothing felt rooted.

I didn't know it at the time, but what I was experiencing was a form of dissociation. A slow, chronic detachment from my own life. A sense that I was living one inch removed from everything. Like I was observing myself from a half-second delay.

Psychologists would later call this a symptom of complex trauma: the mind's way of staying safe when the body no longer feels threatened, but still doesn't feel safe. You're not in danger anymore, but you don't know how to trust the safety either. So you stay suspended. Responsive but uninhabited.

I kept going. I always did. But I remember the specific quiet of that season, the sound of my own breath in a room that felt too still, the way I'd lie on the couch at night with the television on just to hear someone else's voice. The grief wasn't sharp. It was ambient. A kind of gray hum that followed me everywhere.

I didn't tell anyone. Who would I have told? I didn't have the language for it. I didn't know that numbness could be a kind of pain. I didn't know that disconnection could be a trauma response. I just thought I was tired. Unmotivated. Maybe a little broken.

But underneath the numbness was a hunger. I wanted something real. I wanted meaning, the kind that steadies you in a storm. I didn't feel drawn to God, or love, or even myself in any clear way.

Church felt pointless. It felt performative, polished words, tight smiles, the kind of place where everyone seemed to know their lines. I didn't. I didn't want to. I wasn't hunting for doctrine or belonging. I just wanted something that stayed steady when the rest of life shook loose.

There's a story in Matthew about a man who builds on sand. The storm comes, and the whole thing gives way (7:26–27). I used to think that story was about other people, reckless people. Now I see it differently. I used to think that story was about people who chose poorly, who built fragile lives because they were foolish.

But now I wonder if it's also about people like me. People who inherited sand and didn't know they had another option. Some of us learn to build with whatever's on hand, scraps, habits, guesses. You do what you can with the tools you've got.

When things fell apart, I didn't see it as punishment. It just made things visible.

It showed me what I'd built on. The stories I'd inherited. The things I believed without knowing I believed them, about safety, about connection, about how much effort it takes to be worth keeping.

Everything I thought I knew, about what makes a life meaningful, what makes a relationship last, what makes a person good, it all began to erode.

And maybe that was the beginning of grace.

Not the graceful kind that lands like a feather. Sometimes grace doesn't show up with comfort, it rips up the floor so you can finally see what's been holding your weight.

One night stands out. I got home late, the kind of late where traffic bleeds into silence. The apartment was lit, stocked, still. I dropped my keys, stepped into the kitchen, and stood there, staring at nothing. Everything around me said I was okay, fridge humming, lights steady, but my body didn't agree. My skin felt tight. My chest buzzed like I'd outrun something that kept catching up anyway. And I thought, I don't know how to be here. In this life. In this skin. In this room.

I walked to the bathroom. Looked in the mirror. My face looked familiar but distant, like I'd caught up to someone I hadn't met yet.

I didn't feel anything in particular. But I paused. Long enough to notice I was still standing.

That's what the wilderness is like, I think. It's about disorientation. A revealing. And God doesn't always speak in it. Sometimes He just waits with you in the quiet until you remember how to pray.

That year didn't resolve anything. No epiphany. No fresh start. But I started sharing small, personal truths in short, unspectacular ways. A passing comment at work. A muttered sentence in the car. Nothing rehearsed. Just pieces of what I'd been carrying.

And something shifted. The air got thinner. The weight pressed less.

It didn't disappear. But I could move through it. I started to imagine a different kind of life. One with weight. One I could actually feel.

I didn't want the God I was raised to fear, I wanted the one who doesn't walk out when the walls come down.

That stretch of time didn't offer clarity. It taught me something harder: how to stay put when the structure gives way. How to hold still inside the mess. How to stop rebuilding just to avoid the silence.

That's where the real work began.

The First Turning Point

There wasn't a single moment that changed things. No argument. No decision. Just a stretch of time where the air between us started to thin.

The routines stayed the same, but they took more effort. Conversations circled. I could feel something pulling loose, even if neither of us named it.

The closeness we had early on started to fade into logistics and misunderstandings. We argued more than we connected. We weren't building toward anything. We were just coexisting.

We were unsteady long before a child entered the picture. I wanted security, belonging, something to anchor us. In my own flawed logic, I thought a child might provide it, a reason to stay steady, a shared horizon. So together we made the choice, believing it would give us ground to stand on. I became a mother six months before my twenty-sixth birthday. That moment was not only about new life, but about stepping into a story that would reconfigure everything I thought I knew about love, loss, and self.

The relationship stayed tense, but the stakes changed. At some point, it became obvious. I'd been propping things up with sheer effort. When something slipped, I adjusted. When that didn't work, I adjusted again. But the patterns didn't move.

I pushed hard, through tension, through silence, through signals I didn't want to read. And none of it brought us closer.

That was the moment things started to turn. Not a spiritual awakening or emotional breakthrough, just a steady realization that I was burning out trying to hold myself and my relationship upright at the same time. My energy belonged elsewhere. I poured myself into work. Not to please, but to excel. I wanted the leader board. I wanted top-tier bonuses. I wanted to prove, first to myself, and maybe to whoever was watching, that I could master what I touched. I didn't chase praise. I chased precision.

And while that drive stayed sharp, something else began to soften. I stopped trying to manage every interaction. I stopped rearranging myself to keep the peace. I started recognizing what left me empty, and I adjusted accordingly. The pressure didn't fade. I just chose where to place it. I gave it to things I could shape. I stopped giving it to people who wouldn't notice either way.

Romans 12:2 says, *"Be transformed by the renewing of your mind."* I used to hear that as a rule. Now it sounds like permission. Not to think differently in theory, but to choose differently in practice. To put energy where it actually matters. To stop bending toward people who don't see you, and start standing up where you already belong.

The real turning point wasn't about new beliefs. It was about new posture.

Less force. More curiosity.

Less management. More truth.

I didn't start praying again in that stretch. That came later. Spiritually, I felt flat, disconnected, uninterested, uninterested in fixing it. But I started paying closer attention. Not in a soft, reflective way, just in a practical one. What drained me? What steadied me enough to keep going?

I didn't meditate or take up yoga. I chose my time and energy with more precision. I kept notebooks and wrote when I had something to say. I kept the noise down when I could. I turned toward what made sense and pulled back from what didn't.

This wasn't some turning point wrapped in meaning. It was reallocation.

My effort stopped bleeding into places that offered no return. I put it into my child. Into work. Into the version of life I could actually touch with my hands.

These were the markers. In that season, I didn't become someone new. I started to come back to who I had always been.

And for the first time, I allowed that to be enough.

Chapter Three

BECOMING REAL

Humbling Moments and Hidden Grace

Not much changed between us after she came. The tension stayed. The questions didn't go anywhere. What did change, quietly, was how much I stepped in. Filling space, solving things, smoothing over what no one asked me to fix. I wasn't thinking. I was reacting. And it was starting to wear me down. Whatever I thought I was protecting, it wasn't holding. And something quieter, something deeper, was asking me to loosen my hold.

Pregnancy did not soften the strain. Our fights escalated until I packed my bags and left. I was five months along and unemployed, recently let go from the job I had counted on to carry me through maternity leave. The ground gave way all at once, and I had to face the unraveling without a plan.

When I applied for food stamps, they turned me away, said I wasn't eligible without a job. I remember walking out of that office with a surreal mix of disbelief and resolve. I wasn't defeated. I was disoriented. No one prepares you for the moment when your best efforts still aren't enough. But that was the moment I stopped pretending that life could be managed by sheer will.

I didn't stay gone long. After only a few weeks, I returned. The break wasn't final; it was only the first sign of how fragile we were. A few months later, our daughter was born.

What I couldn't name then, but can now, was the quiet presence of grace. Not the tidy kind with bow-wrapped lessons and silver linings. The kind that shows up hidden. Grace in the form of resilience. Grace in the stranger who smiled when I was holding everything together with a frayed thread. Grace in the clarity that rose up in me: You will figure this out.

Psychologists talk about disorienting dilemmas, those moments in adult life when our internal assumptions clash with lived experience. They're not just bumps in the road. They are often the beginning of transformation. Jack Mezirow, who spent his career studying how adults actually grow, believed that change doesn't usually begin with clarity. It begins with disruption.

That's what those months felt like, everything upended, not just on the outside, but inside too. I'd always relied on being capable. I didn't ask for help. I kept things moving. But now I was pregnant, unemployed, and trying to hold together a life I hadn't prepared for. The old rules didn't apply. The girl with the plan was gone. What was left was a woman figuring it out as she went, no map in hand.

Even so, grace was there. Not loudly. But in the mornings I still showed up. In the way I stretched meals, kept my pride, leaned on friends who didn't flinch. Grace didn't pull me out of the mess. It just didn't leave me alone in it.

Scripture doesn't say, "God helps those who help themselves." It says, *"The Lord is near to the brokenhearted and saves the crushed in spirit"* (Psalm 34:18). The entire arc of the Bible leans toward the vulnerable. Toward the humbled. Toward those without pretense or power.

God fed His people with manna, nothing they planted, nothing they stored, nothing they could control. It arrived each morning as provision, not reward. Jesus looked at the poor in spirit and called them blessed, while the world kept celebrating performance. When the crowds asked what God required, He answered with one word: "Believe" (John 6:29). That's it. Not effort. Not achievement. Just trust.

I used to mistake dependence for frailty. In a way, I still see it that way. But I also see it differently now. Dependence is what anchors us to God.

Most of the time, it isn't our titles or roles that form us most deeply. It's the breaks in the system. The losses that stop us. The moments that ask us to start over. Not because pain is holy in itself, but because rupture opens the floor. It gives grace somewhere to land.

Simone Weil wrote, "Grace fills empty spaces, but it can only enter where there is a void to receive it." I didn't want to be empty. I wanted to be competent. But fullness isn't always strength. Sometimes it's armor. It's the illusion that we can do this alone.

It took everything in me to stop performing strength and start receiving mercy.

The gospel isn't a ladder, it's a table. And sometimes the holiest thing we can do is sit down at it with nothing in our hands.

That season taught me to recognize grace not by how bright it felt, but by how near it stayed. It didn't swoop in to fix anything. It just didn't leave. It gave me breath when things got tight. Softened the edge of my anger. Kept me moving when I wasn't sure where I was headed.

Grace doesn't always pour in like light. Sometimes it waits in the dark with you.

That, I've come to believe, is the real work of discipleship. Not looking composed. Not chasing spiritual progress. Just learning to stay honest with God, even when the ground under you disappears.

There is nothing glamorous about being brought low. But there is something sacred about meeting God there.

Not the God of punishment. The God of presence. The One who knows what you need before you ask, and who calls you beloved even when you feel undone.

And when you arrive at that place, exhausted, unguarded, finally available to truth, mercy will meet you there.

It won't ask for credentials.

It will say:

Welcome. You're right on time.

Redefining Success, Redefining Self

After she was born, we found a way to make it work. He worked days, I worked nights. We passed each other in the doorway, handed off the baby, kept things moving. When she was six weeks old, I walked into the company where I would spend most of my career. The need to keep a roof overhead and a life stitched together set me on the path that would define my working years.

It wasn't smooth, but it held. The bills got paid. The house stayed warm. We rented a small place near a park, and most of the time, we were just trying to keep from falling behind. One paycheck away from the car being repossessed. One sick day from having the water shut off.

But we were trying. Together. We were both working. Both parenting. Both hoping this was the beginning of something better.

And maybe it was. But it didn't feel like success.

I had always thought success would come with a kind of internal click, a settling. A moment of deep satisfaction. I wasn't expecting fireworks. But I thought there'd be some sense of arrival. Instead, I was in between, working, parenting, making it through. No title. No raise. Just barely covering bills, raising a baby, and living in a state of constant watchfulness.

It's a strange thing, doing what you're supposed to do and still feeling like something important hasn't clicked. I didn't need more money, necessarily. I needed to feel known. And not just by others, by myself.

I wasn't chasing success. I was chasing belonging.

And I didn't yet know where to find it.

Psychologist Carl Rogers called it the paradox of change: "When I accept myself just as I am, then I can change." But most of us don't get there through acceptance. We get there through adaptation. We manage impressions. We refine our tone. We absorb the message early: if you're impressive, you'll be loved.

I had learned how to be acceptable. I could read a room. I could solve problems. I knew how to say the right thing, soften an edge, disappear the parts of me that didn't quite match. It came naturally. But the more I adjusted, the less rooted I felt. Being useful had always come easy. At some point, I had to ask, who was I actually serving? And why did showing up that way leave me so depleted?

The model of success I grew up with was built on output. You work. You help. You prove your worth. That was the deal.

But over time, it started to break down. All that effort, and still something felt off. Not from burnout, but from the slow realization that I was chasing the wrong thing. It wasn't ambition anymore. It was something else trying to get my attention. Just a quiet unrest I couldn't shake. A different question:

What if being admired isn't the point? What if being real is?

The world doesn't ask you to be real. It asks you to be reliable.

That message clung to me for years.

I was working. Showing up. Carrying my part. The paychecks grew steadier. The work wasn't impressive, but it was steady. I had a schedule, a paycheck, a place to be. It gave me room to breathe. I could see myself staying, not forever, but long enough to build something that felt like mine.

The job itself wasn't the point. What mattered was that something finally held. I didn't have to scramble. I didn't have to pivot or hustle to keep things from falling apart. I could root.

And even then, the question stayed with me:

Is this it?

Or was there a different way to live, one that didn't trade identity for usefulness?

Forgiveness as a Path to Maturity

Around that same time, I knew I had to confront my past if I didn't want to pass it forward. Over the span of those early years, I had three conversations that reshaped my future, one with my father, one with my grandmother, and one with my mother. Each required me to name what had been, to forgive, and to set new boundaries. They were not neat resolutions, but they marked a break from the quiet agreements of my childhood.

I didn't plan them. But I had reached the stage of life where silence felt heavier than truth. I needed to say, out loud, what had shaped me. What had broken something in me. What I still carried, sometimes consciously, sometimes not.

I didn't approach these conversations with anger. I wasn't looking for apologies. I was looking for clarity. For space to name what had never been named.

I told each of them what it felt like to be the child caught in their patterns. What it was like to be three years old and already trying to make sense of abandonment. Already building a story about my worth from their actions and absences. I told them about the expectations I'd had, not just then, but now. As an adult. As a woman trying to piece together where I came from and who I was becoming.

And when I finished speaking, I forgave them.

I forgave my dad for leaving, for the years of absence and the confusion it left behind.

I forgave my grandmother for staying silent when she knew what was happening inside our home.

I forgave my mother, for the volatility, the favoritism, the harshness she called discipline. I told her I would not continue the old pattern of pretending everything was fine. That if we were to have a relationship as adults, it would need to be built on mutual respect and healthy boundaries.

She couldn't accept that. Not fully. And though I grieved her inability to meet me there, I also felt something sacred settle inside me. I had told the truth. I had released the debt. I'd said what needed saying. Not to rewrite the past, but to stop it from defining the present.

For a long time, I believed forgiveness had to come with a feeling. That it didn't really count unless something inside me softened. I kept waiting for that shift, to feel lighter, clearer, free. I journaled. I prayed. I tried to will it into being. Tried to force a release that never came.

But the heaviness didn't lift. The same old loops played in my head. One voice, one look, one careless comment could send me right back, tight in the chest, on edge, ashamed for still carrying it.

It took a long time to learn that forgiveness isn't something you feel first. It's something you choose. And sometimes, you have to choose it while your heart is still catching up.

Scripture never presents forgiveness as something optional or soft. It doesn't promise relief. It asks us to do it anyway, not because it's easy, but because it's the only path that keeps us honest.

Paul puts it plainly in Colossians: "Forgive, as the Lord forgave you." Not because the harm disappears. Not because the other person suddenly understands. But because holding it forever will reshape you, and not in the way you want. Forgiveness matters because it keeps truth from curdling into retaliation.

That's what took me the longest to understand. I thought forgiveness meant dialing down the pain. Swallowing it. Getting quiet enough to seem okay. As if strength meant pretending it didn't leave a mark. But I never believed it meant excusing the harm, or inviting it back in. Some people don't change. Forgiveness is not about giving them another chance to prove that. It's about freeing yourself from the weight of waiting for that day.

Biblical forgiveness doesn't deny harm. It names it. It stands in the truth of it. And then it chooses not to pass the pain forward. Forgiveness is not forgetting. It's remembering without retribution.

I used to think maturity meant composure. Grace under pressure. Wisdom that didn't flinch. But now I see maturity as the ability to hold paradox: to acknowledge what someone did and still wish them well. To grieve what was lost and still release the debt. To say this hurt me without letting that hurt define who I become.

I couldn't do that in my early twenties, I wasn't ready. I could say the words, I forgive you, but I didn't know how to live it. I either held onto resentment or buried it. Either way, it shaped me. Not in honesty, but in reaction.

What I hadn't learned yet was how to forgive without surrendering my right to be angry and still be at peace.

Psychologist Janis Abrahms Spring draws a distinction between cheap forgiveness and real forgiveness. Cheap forgiveness is immediate. It asks nothing of the offender and too much of the wounded. It values peace over truth. Real forgiveness starts when you name the harm and take back your voice. That reframed everything for me.

It meant I didn't have to keep performing okay-ness. I could tell the truth, about what it cost, about what it shaped in me, about how it rewired the way I moved through the world. And only when I stopped minimizing it could I begin to let it go.

Because forgiveness that asks you to lie about the damage isn't forgiveness. It's denial.

There are people I've forgiven who will never hear it. Some never apologized. Some offered apologies, but they didn't risk much. I used to think forgiveness had to happen in relationship, that it needed both people to name the truth. But most of the time, it doesn't unfold like that. It's personal. Quiet. Something you decide when you're finally ready to stop holding it all.

Even Jesus didn't wait for remorse. Hanging on the cross, He said, *"Father, forgive them,"* before anyone admitted to anything. He said, *"Father, forgive them, for they know not what they do"* (Luke 23:34). I used to hear that as impossibly divine. Now I hear it as deeply human. An exhausted, steady refusal to become the harm that was done to Him.

It wasn't acceptance. It was resistance, the kind that holds shape when everything else falls apart. That's the line between trauma and transformation. One keeps you circling the pain. The other lets you move through it without becoming it. It reminds us of who we were all along.

I've come to see my own acts of forgiveness as a form of resistance, too. Not to truth, but to bitterness. Resistance to becoming a mirror of the harm. Resistance to shrinking my life around someone else's sin. Resistance to staying tethered to what I've already handed over to God.

There's a freedom that comes. Not right away. But eventually. When the scar is still there, but the heat has left it. When I can tell the story without collapsing inside it. When I can pray for them, not with clenched teeth, but with open hands.

Not because they deserve it. Because I do.

Forgiveness may not be the goal of every story. Sometimes what's needed first is grief. Or distance. Or a season of rebuilding. But I do believe forgiveness is essential to becoming whole.

Because as long as I cling to what they owe me, I'm still living in the shadow of the harm. And God didn't call me to live in shadow. He called me to live in light.

Forgiveness isn't the end of the story.

But it might be the first breath of a new one.

Naming What Matters Most

At some point, quiet, gradual, you begin to see your life reflect not just what you've done, but what you've allowed. The pace slows. Priorities rearrange themselves. And with that, a different kind of question emerges: What actually matters now?

Not in theory. In practice.

What brings peace? What holds your attention in a way that feels honest? What's still worth tending in this season of your life?

These aren't indulgent questions. They're directional. They tell you where you're living from.

After I had those conversations, with my mother, my father, and my grandmother, I felt something shift. Not in them. In me. I had said what needed saying. Without anger. Without retreat. Offered forgiveness without forgetting. Clarified what kind of relationship I was still willing to build. And in the aftermath, something opened.

Not a clean slate, but a clearing. A space where deeper questions could finally surface.

Adult development theorists describe midlife as a crossroads. A moment of realignment. In Erikson's model, we move from identity-building to legacy-making. At some point, the questions change. It's no longer just about who you are, but what you've been given, and how to hold it well. How to live it with integrity.

Scripture makes room for that shift. Jesus didn't give people bullet points or benchmarks. He asked questions that stopped them in their tracks. That cut past performance and got straight to the core:

What do you want from me?

Why are you afraid?

Do you love me more than these?

He wasn't checking for competence. He was looking for something deeper. He was looking for clarity. For hearts that could name what mattered and follow it.

That's what I'm learning to do. Not chase clarity as a concept, but live into it as a daily rhythm.

Some of the most sacred truths come into focus during ordinary moments. I was probably in the grocery store, grabbing a gallon of milk or reaching for pasta. I don't even remember. Just moving through the usual motions. And then something in me went still.

Not stuck. Just quiet.

It hit me how long it had been since I felt that way, like I was actually inside my own life. Nothing profound. Just enough calm to notice I was there.

From there, I began paying attention. What nourishes? What brings lightness? What allows for depth?

It wasn't a reinvention. It was a noticing.

The feel of a warm cup of coffee in my hands before sunrise. The calm that follows a truth told gently. The ease of time with people who don't require a performance. A child's curiosity. A friend's laughter. A song sung from the belly, not the throat.

These aren't additions to a good life. They are the good life.

Ecclesiastes says it simply: *"Better is a handful of quietness than two hands full of toil and a striving after wind"* (Ecclesiastes 4:6, ESV).

It's not a warning against ambition. It's a reminder to stay aligned. To build a life that's full, but not frantic. The kind of success that doesn't need an audience. The kind that feels like peace.

The gospel doesn't chase more. It draws us into relationship. Into presence.

We weren't made to hustle our way into worth. We are called to dwell.

Naming what matters isn't about scripting the rest of your life. It's about trusting the life already forming beneath your feet. It's about recognizing the fruit of the Spirit where it naturally grows, in small exchanges, in honest prayer, in presence that needs no proof.

It's also about recalibration. Choosing what to tend, and what to release.

That might look like carving out time for what actually lifts you. Making space to be curious again. Letting your energy go toward the slow, often quiet work of becoming more fully yourself.

When you name what matters, everything else can shift into place. Not thrown out. Just no longer confused for the point.

These days, I keep moving toward simplicity, not out of lack, but out of loyalty. I want less noise. More depth. A life that means something because I paid attention to it. Intention over image. I'm drawn to lives that are not loud but full. People who bless others without spectacle. Spaces that hold silence without rushing to fill it.

The things that matter most to me now are not new. They've been there all along, waiting for me to notice.

Slow mornings, when nothing demands you. Friends who tell the truth and don't expect you to perform. Time to be alone without needing a reason. The kind of home that doesn't ask more of you than you have to give. A way of living that doesn't require the mask.

Jesus said, *"Where your treasure is, there your heart will be also"* (Matthew 6:21). I used to hear that as a warning. Now I receive it as a compass.

If I want my heart to root somewhere solid, I have to name the treasure. Not just believe in it, but live by it.

So I name it.

Stillness. Presence. Kindness that doesn't seek credit. Faith that holds steady. Courage to speak when it's costly. Joy that doesn't require an audience.

And when I name these things, I feel my life begin to rise toward them.

To become real is not to be exposed. It is to be seen in full. Known in truth. Aligned in soul.

This is the invitation of maturity, not a ladder to climb, but a homecoming. To the person God has been shaping beneath all the roles and rhythms. To the values that have been stitched into our spirit from the beginning.

Naming what matters isn't a declaration. It's a discipline. A way of staying honest with yourself about what you're building, and what you're no longer willing to carry.

I don't have it all defined. But I know what feels steady. I know what pulls me back to center. And that's enough to keep going.

ACT II: BELONGING

THE ACT OF APPLYING

Chapter Four
THE WORK OF LOVE

Learning to Love Without Losing Myself

Love never felt straightforward. I didn't trust it enough to relax into it. I approached it indirectly, careful not to step too far in without knowing the way out. By the time I had the chance to love freely, instinct was already in charge, an instinct built on watching for shifts, anticipating change, and preparing for retreat. I approached love the way some people approach deep water, with caution, with one foot still on the shore. Even when it reached toward me, I looked for what might come next. I listened for the subtle shifts, the drop in temperature before the break.

Growing up, affection wasn't something I could count on. Some days there was softness. Other days, distance settled in without warning. I adjusted early, long before I had language for what I was responding to. A slight change in tone or posture was enough to let me know how the day might go. I shaped myself around the mood in the room, picking up what wasn't said and acting accordingly.

Sometimes I was welcomed in, and at other times I felt like I was too much. The rules kept shifting. I just learned to stay one step ahead of the fallout. And I learned, by repetition, not instruction, that love was not something I could trust to stay. So I did what many children do in unstable homes: I adapted. I became attentive, responsible, useful. Quiet when needed. Fierce when cornered. And in that environment, survival often looked like over-functioning.

By the time I reached my twenties, I had no template for intimacy that didn't require some form of shape-shifting. I knew how to be "the strong one," how to be essential, how to anticipate needs before they were spoken. But I didn't yet know how to be fully known and still feel safe. Or chosen. Or held.

That made love complicated.

When I met the man who would eventually become the father of my daughter, I wanted love that could last. I wanted family. But I also wanted control. Not out of ego, but out of fear. I believed that if I could manage the environment, keep the peace, meet expectations, I could protect what I was building.

By the time our marriage and parenting were underway, the deeper question pressed in: what did love really require of me? Not more effort, not more management, but something truer. That became the work of those years.

In some ways, it did. I became more tender. I paid attention to things I used to miss. But real love, the kind that reorders your inner life, doesn't come from trying harder. It depends on how honest you're willing to be. And back then, I wasn't used to bringing my full self to anything.

Motherhood stripped away the layers I had learned to hide behind. The careful composure, the polished responses, the belief that I could manage my way into safety, none of it held under the sleepless nights and relentless needs of a newborn. I was raw, my fear and irritation rising to the surface faster than I could push them down. In that unraveling, something unexpected began: a slow and reluctant honesty. For the first time, I could no longer perform my way into belonging.

And in the middle of that mess, something shifted. I started to understand that love isn't something you manage into place. It doesn't always respond to effort the way we're told it will. Sometimes it asks you to just stay, to be fully present with what's happening, even when it's messy or uncomfortable.

Letting someone close felt risky. It still does. Because underneath it all, there was a question I couldn't shake: if someone really saw me, what I carried, what I wanted, what I hadn't figured out, would they still want to stay?

That question didn't belong to one relationship. It followed me everywhere. It didn't just belong to my marriage. It surfaced in how I showed up as a mother, how I held friendships, how I prayed.

For years, I believed love had to be earned with effort. If I could get it right, stay calm, be generous, say the wise thing, I could keep the connection. That belief ran deep. But something else was beginning to stir beneath it.

"We love because He first loved us." (1 John 4:19, NIV)

That verse resonated. It undid the math I'd been living by. I'd always thought love came second, after effort, after sacrifice, after getting it right. But this said love came first. Already given. Already present. Not earned. Just... true.

But that didn't land all at once. It took years. It took disillusionment, and loss, and the slow unraveling of every strategy I'd used to belong. I'd spent most of my life believing love had to be secured. That being easy, agreeable, available, that was the price of connection.

And then, something shifted. It started when my daughter was invited to church by a friend from school. She wanted to go, so I said yes. Eventually my husband and I joined her. We'd sit in the back, mostly quiet, mostly watching. But something in me softened.

A few years later, she came to me and said she wanted to be baptized. We talked about it. Prayed. She was ready. And somewhere in that conversation, I realized I was too. I had always felt the absence of God, assumed it was mine to carry. I'd been sprinkled as a baby, but this felt different. Intentional. Chosen.

We were baptized together. Mother and daughter, side by side.

That was the doorway.

After that, I couldn't get enough of Scripture. I read it with fresh eyes, eyes that were hungry, not for rules, but for relationship. I saw that the Bible wasn't just instruction, it was love, revealed over and over again. Love given first. Not because of worthiness, but because of grace.

That was the beginning of the return.

And from that place, love started to look different. I stopped pulling away when something hurt. When I went quiet, it wasn't to hide, it was to stay present with what was real. I began to say what I meant, even when it felt risky. I stopped confusing peace with silence. I stopped disappearing to make others more comfortable.

I wanted relationships where I didn't have to leave parts of myself behind. Where I could bring my whole self, honest, flawed, still becoming, and be received.

In one Gospel account, a man asks Jesus which commandment matters most... *"'Love the Lord your God with all your heart and with all your soul and with all your mind.'... And the second is like it: 'Love your neighbor as yourself.'"* (Matthew 22:37–39, NIV)

For years, I focused on the first part. But the second part holds the secret. As yourself. Love for others and love for self are not in competition. They rise together.

To love myself wasn't rebellion. It was alignment. I began to believe that the person God had shaped in me was already deserving of tenderness, because grace had already claimed me.

This stretch of my life, the slow, sacred work of learning to love, wasn't about seeking perfection in someone else. It was about returning to a way of loving that didn't ask me to go missing.

It invited truth. It asked me to remain soft without losing my shape.

To trust that love, in its truest form, doesn't require our disappearance.

It welcomes us home.

Marriage and the Myth of Completion

We were a family long before we ever made it official.

In the world I came from, it wasn't strange to build a life before making it official. Marriage carried assumptions, about roles, permanence, performance, that didn't always reflect what we were living. But we had a home. A child. A rhythm. We cooked, argued, shared bills, made up, showed up. It looked settled from the outside. And for a while, that was enough.

But the truth is, our relationship was never the calm kind I pictured. We moved through cycles, disturbance, then peace, then back again. Long stretches where something always felt slightly off-kilter. I kept waiting for it to settle, for the kind of ease I imagined marriage would bring. It never fully arrived.

Still, I wanted to believe in what we had. I wanted it to last. And at some point, I began to feel that what we needed wasn't more effort, it was blessing. I thought maybe naming it before God would ground it. That if we could mark our commitment in sacred language, it might steady what had never quite been still.

When we said our vows, that's what I was reaching for. Not formality. Not approval. Just a way to honor what we had built, and to ask God to hold what we couldn't seem to hold alone.

But eventually I learned something I hadn't known to look for: that covenant is not the same as cure.

I had imagined that marriage might soften the tension we carried. That commitment might draw us closer. That showing up faithfully would deepen the intimacy between us. I thought that doing the right thing would bring about the right feeling.

But the ache didn't ease. And the distance didn't close.

We were committed. We stayed. We raised our daughter. We endured the usual storms, lost jobs, family deaths, tight finances. We knew how to function as a unit. But something essential began to drift. Not in one sharp rupture, but in the slow, silent way people start living beside each other instead of with.

And I began to feel it in my body. A kind of slow shrinking. There wasn't some dramatic breaking point. Just a slow fading. My voice got quieter. My wants got smaller. The roles were still there, wife, mother, partner, but the woman inside them didn't feel present anymore.

I didn't hold it against him. He was good to me in the ways he knew how. He was consistent. Loyal. But we were moving in different directions, even as we kept sharing a life.

I wanted stretch. I wanted depth. I wanted to keep becoming. He wanted things to stay familiar. To hold steady. To go back to something that felt safe.

Neither of us was wrong. We were simply walking in different directions.

The world had told me that marriage would complete the story. That two would become one, and the search would be over. I had taken in the message from all directions, films, church pulpits, the quiet comments of women a little further down the road. The idea was clear: marriage, done well, would offer clarity. A kind of inner settling. The sense that you had arrived.

But the restlessness stayed with me.

I asked God to help me find peace in the life we were building. To make me content where I stood. What I heard in return wasn't comfort. At least, not right away. It felt more like a quiet directive: listen closer. Come back to yourself. To the voice you learned to quiet. The one that told the truth before you started editing it for everyone else.

Esther Perel says we want our partner to be both our anchor and our wave. I feel that. I wanted to feel held, but I also wanted to keep moving. I wasn't craving chaos, I just didn't want to disappear inside someone else's idea of stability. But in our dynamic, anchoring meant staying still. And staying still began to cost more than I could keep paying.

Faith taught me to honor covenant. And I still do. But covenant must make room for transformation. A vow doesn't mean much if it asks you to disappear to keep it.

"Let your yes be yes and your no, no." (Matthew 5:37)

It sounded like a warning, don't back out, don't break the promise. But now it sounds like something else. A call to be honest, to speak plainly, and to stop pretending something's there when there isn't.

I meant it when I said yes, but the life that yes belonged to changed. I changed. And I could be wrong, but I don't think God asks us to stay loyal to something that's no longer true, not even in the name of faithfulness.

I still believe in vows. In wrestling. In choosing one another through seasons of uncertainty. But I also believe in resurrection. And resurrection often begins with a death. Some covenants complete their work, not because we didn't love well enough, but because the purpose they served has been fulfilled.

What marriage taught me is this: love and liberation are not the same thing. You can love someone and still know that the life you've created together is no longer where your soul can breathe.

For a while, things got better. After the wedding, there was a sense of intention between us. We were trying. I held onto that. I wanted to believe the commitment had created a shift, and for a time, it felt like it had.

But over the years, the patterns returned. The tension. The imbalance. The quiet slide back into something that looked like partnership but didn't feel like shared weight. I found myself holding more and more, managing the home, making the decisions, carrying the emotional labor. I wasn't disappearing. I was shouldering everything.

Instead of walking side by side, I felt like I was steering a ship he'd climbed aboard. He was kind. He was present. But he had settled in as a passenger. And I was the one charting the course, keeping us afloat, making sure nothing fell apart.

That's not how it's meant to be.

Scripture says, "Submit to one another out of reverence for Christ." (Ephesians 5:21)

That's the part that kept echoing. One another. Mutual care. Shared responsibility. The kind of love that asks both people to carry, to listen, to serve.

I didn't walk away from marriage because I stopped believing in covenant. I walked away because I started believing that covenant doesn't mean carrying it all alone. And that God's vision for relationship includes both people standing up, showing up, and growing.

We didn't fail. We finished.

And even in the ending, there was grace.

We had given each other what we could. We had learned. We had built. And when it was time to release, we found the strength to do so.

The myth says marriage completes you.

But the truth, the truth that set me free, is this: only God does.

Parenting as Surrender and Stewardship

Becoming a mother reshaped me, not all at once, but in slow, reverent increments. Love didn't rush in. It arrived carefully, after grief had cleared the ground.

Two years before she was born, I lost a daughter in the final stretch of pregnancy, seven and a half months along. That loss left its mark. I carried it quietly, but it changed how I approached everything that came next. When my living daughter arrived, healthy and whole, I thanked God with trembling hands. I knew she was a gift. But I also knew gifts could be taken. So I loved her carefully, with a kind of cautious reverence. I met every need, tended every cry, but the emotional bond took time to grow roots.

Very early on, I handed her over. Not to the world, but to God.

In the stillness of those first days, I spoke aloud what my heart already knew: "She is Yours first. Teach me how to raise her. Guide me so I can guide her. Help me hold her loosely, and trust You completely." That wasn't just a prayer. It became the architecture of how I mothered.

I didn't expect motherhood to fix anything in me. I had already stopped asking for that. But I did expect to do it differently than how I was raised. I wanted to build a home where warmth outshined volatility. Where truth was spoken without cruelty. Where presence mattered more than performance.

Even still, I was learning love in real time.

In the beginning, my care for her was rooted in responsibility. She needed me, utterly. And I showed up, utterly. Over time, that dutiful presence deepened into joy. I saw the shape of her spirit, perceptive, playful, deeply feeling. I marveled at her early wisdom. And slowly, the love I had been guarding flooded in. It became vast, resonant, secure. No longer reactive. No longer afraid. Just real.

From the beginning, I understood: she came through me, not from me. She was mine to care for, but not to keep. I was responsible for her development, not for her future.

That distinction mattered. It still does.

Stewardship became the word that made sense. It wasn't my job to turn her into a mini-me. It wasn't my job to protect her from every heartache. She was mine to guide. To bless. To help form with a light touch and a steady heart.

"Train up a child in the way they should go, and when they are old they will not depart from it." (Proverbs 22:6, KJV)

That verse grew more expansive the longer I mothered her. I no longer heard it as a call to discipline or direction, but to discernment. The way they should go. Not the way I might have gone. Not the version of life I wished someone had carved out for me. But the way God designed her to move through this world.

My job wasn't to define her. It was to discover her. To pay close enough attention to notice who she already was, and to bless that.

There were seasons of ease, and seasons that stretched us. Sometimes she pulled away. Sometimes I did. There were days when I didn't know what she needed. But even then, I trusted the relationship more than the moment. I stayed available. I stayed soft. And I let space do its quiet work.

I never wanted her to orbit around me. I wanted her to become fully herself. So I let her go, bit by bit, without guilt or guilt-tripping... or at least I tried to. I celebrated her independence because I had been preparing for it from the start. That was the promise I had made in the beginning, that she belonged first to God.

When she reached adulthood, our relationship shifted again. She didn't need direction anymore. She needed witness. A place to bring her questions. When she had something to share, she brought it to me in her own time. I didn't press for more than she was ready to give. My role was to hold the space, steady, spacious, honest. I didn't always get it right, but I stayed. And over the years, that consistency created something solid between us.

Marriage had already started to expose my blind spots, but nothing revealed them as sharply as parenting. Parenting taught me to pay close attention, not to control, but to notice. To keep hold of my own sense of self while honoring hers. To trust her unfolding without needing to shape every part of it.

She turned to me when she needed grounding. My job was to remain steady and real, and to be someone she could count on without having to carry.

And when it was time for her to step into her life fully, I let her go without resistance. She had become a woman I respected. Releasing her didn't feel like an ending. It felt complete.

If parenting has a sacred task, it is this: to lead with care, to hold with intention, and to witness with love as someone becomes fully themselves.

To parent from stewardship is to say: I will honor your becoming. I will care for what has been entrusted to me. And when the time comes, I will release what was mine to hold for a time and trust that the love we built will carry on, finding its way into the next season of her life.

The Slow Art of Staying

Staying is a sacred act of presence.

For a long time, I believed staying was the answer. I stayed through the tension. Through the disappointments. Through long seasons where peace was hard to come by. I kept thinking, if I just hold steady, if I ride this out, it'll get better.

So I held it all. The house, the emotions, the schedules, the faith. I stayed small so the family could stay whole. I told myself it was devotion. I told myself it was strength.

But over time, that kind of staying started to feel more like survival than presence.

What I began to understand is that real staying isn't about absorbing everything. It's not about carrying more than your share or managing someone else's growth. It's not silent suffering.

Staying, in its truest form, asks for clarity. It asks you to discern what's yours to hold and what's not. It invites presence, not performance. Honesty, not endurance for its own sake.

Eventually, I stopped calling it faithfulness when what I was doing was over-functioning. I stopped equating self-sacrifice with spiritual maturity.

Because staying, when it's rooted in truth, makes space for both people to show up fully. And if only one person is doing the work, it's not staying, it's slowly breaking down.

As a mother, staying looked like holding steady while she found her own rhythm. I didn't always have the right words, but I gave her space. When she pulled back, I stayed available. That gave her room to trust her own becoming, and gave me a front-row seat to witness it.

Friendship took on a quieter shape. I stopped thinking of it as grand gestures and instead focused on what held over time, a quick check-in, a quiet offer of help, the kind of care that doesn't draw attention to itself. Just being there, without trying to solve anything.

Faith, too, asked something similar. I didn't always have clarity. I didn't always have words. Still, I returned, through silence, through drought, through longing I couldn't fully name. Prayer became less about saying the right thing and more about staying in the conversation. Even when I had nothing to offer but breath, I showed up. Because presence itself became the offering.

"Lo, I am with you always, even unto the end of the world." (Matthew 28:20, KJV)

Always. That word has become a place I can rest. Not conditional. Not earned. Just promised.

That's the love I model my staying after.

Psychologists call it earned security, trust built through consistent, safe connection over time. In parenting, in friendship, in marriage, in community, staying creates the conditions for that trust to grow. But it only holds when presence is mutual. When staying is chosen, not performed. Shared, not carried alone.

I've also come to see staying as essential to purpose. Whether in work, calling, or place, when we remain long enough, something new begins to surface. We start to notice what we missed when we were rushing. The deeper textures. The quiet rhythms. The way repetition, done with care, begins to shape both the work and the worker.

That slower rhythm teaches us to stop grasping for control. To let go of the need to know exactly where the road leads. It creates space for trust, to believe that something meaningful is forming, even if we can't yet see its shape. Love grows best in that kind of soil. Quiet. Unforced. Given room.

To stay with integrity means staying awake. It means noticing where your presence brings life and choosing to root there. It means offering your time and energy where something mutual can take hold, where joy has space to stretch, where both people, or the work itself, are still growing.

Every time we choose to stay, with a person, a purpose, a prayer, we enter into the deep work of love. And each time we return, even after drifting, we lay down another layer of trust within ourselves.

Staying says: I believe this matters.

I believe something good can grow here.

I believe I can be fully present, without vanishing in the process.

It isn't glamorous. But it is holy.

Chapter Five

CAREER AND CALLING

Work That Builds or Breaks

Before I ever had a job with a title or a paycheck, I had a pull.

I couldn't have named it then, but I was already wired to think in systems. I wanted to understand how things connected. I noticed patterns, solved puzzles in my head, and saw the consequences of small decisions before anyone spoke them aloud. Even in childhood, I was tracking complexity, relational, emotional, logistical. While others were reacting, I was already scanning for structure.

I wasn't trying to control anything. It was more about clarity.

Clarity became my compass. Especially when life felt unstable, I relied on my ability to observe, anticipate, and adjust. That instinct stayed with me. It was still there the day I started at the company where I would eventually build a decades-long career.

Back then, I was no one special. I entered near the bottom, with no title to speak of and nothing flashy on my résumé. I came in ready to work. No expectations beyond earning my paycheck and keeping my head down. But even then, I was paying attention.

Meetings were short and hierarchical, task updates, procedural reviews, assignments handed down. There was no roundtable discussion, no brainstorming. We weren't invited to contribute insights. We were expected to listen, take notes, and follow the documented process. If something didn't fit the model, we escalated it upward. That was the rule.

I understood structure. I worked well inside it. But I also saw where it broke down. People followed the process, but when they asked why, the answer was always the same: "That's how the sponsor wants it." End of discussion. No curiosity. No adjustments. Just compliance.

I'd always respected the system, but that didn't mean I trusted it. Not everything that ran smoothly was actually working.

People complained, often. But nothing changed.

Even so, I kept showing up. I worked through long seasons that felt more like maintenance than movement. Same routines. Same rhythms. But I stayed with it. Not because it was exciting, because it was mine to do.

When openings came, I stepped forward. One application at a time. No urgency, but no hesitation either. I didn't force the pace. I just kept growing into what was next.

With each new role, something expanded. My skills sharpened. My confidence solidified. I began to see more clearly what I was capable of carrying.

The promotions came over time. Not fast, not flashy, but real. I didn't draw attention to myself. I focused on the work, paid attention to the details most people overlooked. Anticipating needs became second nature, solving problems before they reached the surface.

With time, trust built around me. I wasn't the loudest in the room, but I paid attention. I caught the details others passed over, stayed with the work until it was done right. People knew I would follow through. No chasing required.

Eventually, with more responsibility came a broader field of vision. Patterns I hadn't seen before began to take shape. The way things connected, or didn't, stood out more clearly. I began to see how departments drifted past one another, how systems overlapped without really speaking to each other. Issues that kept resurfacing because no one had the bandwidth, or the authority, to fix them. The answers weren't hidden. They just weren't being heard. I saw places where things could work better. I had ideas. What I didn't have was a real way to voice them. In a culture that prized hierarchy, insight from my level wasn't often invited. It rewarded compliance. I wasn't discouraged, but I wasn't empowered either.

That's what this section is about. Not job titles or promotions. Not even success, exactly. It's about what work does to a soul over time. How it shapes your sense of presence. How it asks for more than just labor, how it starts to form or fragment your sense of self.

Some jobs built me. They gave me steady ground, room to observe, opportunities to learn from patterns. Even in rigid environments, I kept noticing where things could flow more cleanly, where systems didn't talk to each other, where human insight got lost in procedural noise. Those roles helped me clarify my voice, even if I wasn't using it out loud yet.

Other jobs stretched me in ways I couldn't name then. The structure was clear, the expectations were set, but my inner life was changing. I was developing not just skills, but instincts. I began to know what worked even before someone confirmed it. That was its own kind of building. Quiet, internal, long.

I didn't always know how to describe what I felt after work. There were days I left full of energy, days I left depleted. But the difference always came down to this: had I been allowed to bring my whole mind into the room, or just my obedience?

Work builds you when it aligns with your internal structure. When your design, your precision, your endurance, your discernment, finds room to move. When what you naturally offer has value. When you're not performing usefulness but inhabiting it.

Work breaks you when the form is fixed but your soul is shifting. When you're asked to complete tasks without context. When you're invited to participate but not contribute. When you know what's possible but there's no space to say it.

And sometimes, work does both. You're being shaped and stretched. You're growing in competence while remaining unrecognized for your insight. It doesn't flatten you, but it asks you to carry something quietly.

That, too, is a kind of holy preparation.

"The Lord God took the man and put him in the garden of Eden to work it and keep it" (Genesis 2:15, ESV). Long before the Fall, there was work. Not toil, not drudgery, but purpose. Stewardship. Participation in the life of the world. God didn't hand us busywork. He gave us the work of tending, of engaging what's in front of us with care and attention, shaping it slowly into something that reflects His character. We were made to participate, not just perform.

But much of what we now call work has been stripped of that intention. Systems lean toward measurement. At some point, the shape of vocation starts to shift. What began as meaningful work gets redefined by output, how much you've done, how quickly, how visibly. The language around it changes, too. Productivity replaces purpose. Efficiency becomes the goal.

For a while, it can feel like progress. The structure gives a sense of movement, like something's being built. But eventually you notice: meaning doesn't always follow the checklist. And it rarely shows up in the reports. Sometimes it takes root in the pauses, in the work that doesn't get noticed, in the parts no one's tracking. Value isn't always something you can measure.

You can spend years inside a system and still wonder, "Is any of this mine to carry?"

Psychologist Barry Schwartz, in Why We Work (2015), found that most people don't crave ease, they crave meaning. Autonomy. Contribution. Even in highly structured roles, what we want most is to know that our labor matters. That we are not just part of a process, but part of something that lives beyond procedure.

Midlife doesn't create discontent. It gives it shape. The questions come into focus. The energy you once had for proving thins out. You start asking different things:

- What is being built here?
- Is my presence creating change?
- Am I becoming more of who I am?

I had already learned the weight of Jesus' words: "*Where your treasure is, there your heart will be also*" (Matthew 6:21). In earlier years, the verse revealed what I clung to for security. Now, in the context of career and calling, I could see the same truth at work but in different context. Treasure here doesn't mean currency. It means investment. Time. Presence. What you pour yourself into. Over time, your heart settles there. So it matters what you build. It matters what you give your hours to.

Some forms of labor deepen your courage. Others deepen your caution. Either way, work is always shaping something in you.

But grace enters even here.

Even in roles where your voice isn't invited, God sees what you're carrying. Even when the structure is stiff, the soul can remain soft. Even if your name isn't on the agenda, your integrity lives in the work.

You don't need a perfect environment to become who you were made to be. You need a steady willingness to stay awake inside the life you've been given, and a readiness to respond when God opens the next door.

You'll know it when it comes.

Not because of the title.

But because something in you will breathe more freely.

Ambition, Obedience, and False Measures

I've been ambitious my whole life, though I didn't call it that for a long time.

In the world I came from, ambition wasn't framed as strength. It was something to temper. A woman with drive could too easily be mistaken for difficult. Or arrogant. Or discontent. So I learned to dress it differently. I called it responsibility. I said I was reliable. Hardworking. I framed my effort as obedience, to God, to family, to duty. And some of it was. But not all of it.

There was a part of me that longed to rise. To breathe. And yes, to stand out. To stop worrying about money. To be seen for more than just endurance. To speak in a room without having to earn the right every time.

I didn't call it ambition, but it probably was. I needed to keep moving forward because the cost of standing still was too great. Poverty. Dependence. Disregard. I had known all three. And I wasn't going back.

But beneath that survival instinct was something deeper: a calling that hadn't yet found its language. Something in me already knew I was made to build, not just withstand. That the way I thought, strategic, structured, systems-oriented, wasn't just functional. It was purposeful.

It wasn't about titles, but I wanted my work to matter, and to be seen.

And for a while, I was getting there. Slowly, steadily. One promotion at a time. I had worked my way into a mid-level role. My name was beginning to carry weight. The learning curve was still steep, but I was finding my stride. And then, just like that, the ladder cracked beneath me.

A repetitive motion injury knocked me out of the climb. Suddenly, I was dropped down two grades. Reassigned. Reboxed. Told what I could no longer do. My knowledge didn't vanish, but it didn't count anymore. My expertise didn't disappear, but it wasn't called on.

The timeline shifted. I was looking at one last opportunity for advancement before retirement. The years I had spent moving up were compressed into a much smaller frame. There was no sudden unraveling, just a quiet turning point I couldn't push aside.

I was facing a clock. Retirement eligibility was close enough to see, but not close enough to coast. I had one shot left. One last opportunity to position myself for work that made use of what I knew, how I thought, and who I was becoming.

So I went back to school, enrolled in a technical program, still working full-time, and still raising my daughter. I didn't have time to think about whether I was too old or too tired or too late. I had a window, and I meant to climb through it before it closed.

The push was intense. But there was clarity in it. The work I was training for made sense to me on a cellular level. I could see patterns, anticipate logic, solve problems others hadn't seen yet. It didn't feel like striving, it felt like alignment.

I crossed the stage for my degree the same year my daughter crossed hers. And when I stepped into the new role shortly after, I didn't feel like a different person. I felt like I'd finally stepped into the shape I'd been growing toward all along. What drove me then wasn't the desire to rise. It was the determination to stay visible. To hold on to what I'd built. To keep from being pushed to the edges before I was ready to go.

In the church, I had learned to associate obedience with surrender. To be wary of ambition. Too much desire could be mistaken for pride. I believed that for years. Still do, to a point. But I've also seen how obedience gets twisted into a kind of silence. Especially for women. Especially for those of us who learned early not to take up space.

It's possible to obey and disappear at the same time.

I followed the rules. I respected the chain of command. I waited for recognition that never came. I didn't challenge decisions that misused my time or ignored my insight. I smiled when I wanted to speak. I stayed in places that no longer fit because I thought that's what faithfulness looked like. Until I didn't.

Eventually, I began to see it more clearly. Some of what I called obedience was just avoidance. Avoiding conflict. Avoiding disappointment. Avoiding the truth that I wanted more, not more acclaim, but more authority over my own path. More freedom to use what I knew. More room to be honest about what I could still become.

The issue wasn't ambition. The issue was how I had been taught to frame it.

I didn't grow up thinking ambition was a bad thing. I knew I was wired for leadership. It came naturally. What I didn't expect was how often that made people uncomfortable. There were moments, specific ones, where I was shut down. Not because I wasn't capable, but because I wasn't wanted in that space.

Still, the drive didn't go away. I kept showing up. Kept trying.

I told myself God would elevate me in His time. And I believed that, mostly. But looking back, I can see how that belief sometimes became a shield. A way to protect myself from the risk of saying what I really wanted, and being denied again.

Scripture doesn't shame ambition. It invites us to align it. *"Whatever you do, work at it with all your heart, as working for the Lord, not for human masters,"* Paul writes in Colossians 3:23 (NIV). The question isn't whether you're driven. The question is what's driving you.

Ambition starts to blur when it reaches outward too often. When it looks for validation instead of alignment. When the effort becomes more about being seen than about staying true. It wears you down that way, always performing, always hoping someone will notice.

But ambition can also hold steady when it's shaped by calling. When it comes from something planted deep, it becomes a companion through the harder seasons. Even when roles shift. Even when titles fall away. That core sense of direction doesn't disappear.

Obedience, at its heart, is meant to connect us more fully to God, not to flatten our voice or silence our instincts. It isn't about erasing who we are. It's about bringing that identity into clearer focus.

Obedience like that changes how we listen. It invites us to pay attention to how we've been shaped. To notice the instincts that carry peace. The moments when the Spirit leans close and nudges us forward, not loudly, but with weight. You sense the direction before you can explain it.

Calling doesn't always feel like clarity. Sometimes it feels like weight. Like something you're meant to carry, but not yet equipped to lift. You move toward it anyway, through resistance, through silence, trusting that faithfulness will do what force can't.

It doesn't unfold all at once. It takes shape as you go.

When I look back on that stretch, the limits, the change in pace, the shift in direction, I don't feel regret. What I remember most is the steadiness. I stayed in the room. I kept showing up. I showed up with what I had and asked God to bless what was still in my hands.

That's the part I'm proud of.

Not the titles.

Not the steps I climbed.

But the moments I kept going when there was no guarantee I'd get another shot.

Ambition didn't fail me. It kept me honest. It reminded me that I still had something to give. That I was still becoming.

And God never asked me to make myself smaller. He asked me to be faithful. To speak when it was time. To take the next step when the opportunity came. To trust that what He planted in me had not expired.

There's courage in naming your desire. Not as entitlement, but as offering.

So yes, I applied again. I rose again. I stewarded the time that was left.

And I did it with full awareness: ambition can serve the soul when it's led by the Spirit.

You don't need permission to bring your whole self to the table.

Just readiness.

Midlife Questions and Recalibration

You think the questions will stop once you "arrive." After the promotion. After the degree. After the roof gets fixed and the fridge stays full. After the years of showing up.

But midlife doesn't silence the questions. It sharpens them.

I was in my mid-forties when the shift began. Steady and insistent, like water slowly changing the shape of rock. From the outside, things looked solid. I had a job. A long marriage. A daughter nearing graduation. I had kept my head down and made things work. But something inside me had started to ask different questions.

The climb had slowed after the injury. I'd lost ground, dropped two grades, watched years of progress vanish with one diagnosis. I knew I had one last shot at promotion before retirement eligibility. That kind of clarity doesn't leave much room for self-deception. It makes the questions sharp and urgent.

I left my marriage.

We had shared a long season together. Built a life. Raised a child. But the foundation that had once held was now too narrow. He wanted comfort. Familiar rhythms. I was hungering for something else, expansion, expression, the freedom to keep growing. Staying would have required shrinking. And I couldn't do that anymore.

By the time I stepped into the systems analyst role, I knew I was exactly where I was meant to be. The title fit, but more than that, the work fit. I was doing what I was built to do, untangling problems, translating complexity, building order out of mess. But it didn't come with ease. With new authority came new weight. It didn't feel like the end of anything. If anything, it felt like the beginning.

Around that same time, I started asking questions at work that no one else was asking. Policy questions. Equity questions. Questions about how decisions were made and who they impacted. I didn't do it to stir things up. I did it because I couldn't not.

People started paying attention. Especially those higher up. It wasn't that I spoke often, it's that when I did, I didn't flinch. I named what others avoided. I asked questions that didn't have safe answers. I stayed calm, stayed focused, stayed with the real issue.

I didn't set out to join the labor movement. I wasn't looking for a fight. I was trying to make sense of things that didn't add up.

But once you start saying what others are afraid to, something shifts. That's often where leadership begins, not with a title, but with a truth no one else wants to touch.

Developmental psychologist Erik Erikson described this season as a pivot toward purpose, toward building something that holds weight beyond the moment. Something that endures. A refusal to coast. Not a crisis, but a commitment.

Midlife doesn't demand reinvention. It asks for clarity.

What am I building?

Where is it headed?

And am I still becoming in the process?

For some, that clarity means stepping away from old roles. For others, it means reentering them with a different posture. Either way, the old metrics no longer hold. Prestige doesn't satisfy. Performance no longer earns the same high. What matters now is coherence. Does my life still reflect what I value?

You start to notice your own body more. How you brace before meetings. How your energy shifts in certain conversations. How you scan job postings, not seriously, just steadily, like you're checking for a way out that doesn't betray what you've built.

You're not restless. You're aware.

And the questions come, clear and holy:
- Does this still feel like mine?
- Am I growing here?
- What is being asked of me, and do I want to offer it?

Even Jesus paused. Even He withdrew. After His baptism, He entered the wilderness, not to escape, but to prepare. After He fed thousands, He didn't stay to soak up praise. He retreated to pray (Mark 6:46). Jesus didn't respond on impulse. He didn't respond to urgency the way we often do. He stepped back when clarity was needed, found quiet, waited for the moment that felt right to move again. That kind of rhythm stayed with me, even when I didn't have words for it yet.

The shift wasn't sudden. But over time, I started to feel the weight of roles I hadn't consciously chosen, expectations I'd inherited, agreed to, absorbed without question. I'd said yes because I could, not because I should.

Letting go didn't mean leaving. It meant getting honest. Showing up with less pretending. Refusing to perform peace I didn't feel. Relearning how to serve without disappearing.

I began loosening my grip on certain roles, ones I'd taken on without ever really choosing them. The kind of responsibilities you say yes to because you're capable, not because you're called. I wasn't walking away from my life. I was trying to live it with more honesty.

Eventually I stopped forcing myself to meet expectations that no longer made sense. Recalibrating didn't mean leaving the space. It meant showing up with a different posture.

I started to speak when I had something solid to say, and stayed quiet when I didn't. I let silence do its work. When I did speak, I was direct. Not to stir things up, but to ground the room again.

I wasn't looking for affirmation. I was looking for alignment.

And slowly, that shift brought clarity. Not all at once, but enough. I started to see where my voice mattered most. What I could still carry. What was no longer mine.

What we forget is that purpose matures.

Sometimes it deepens, sometimes it narrows, sometimes it changes shape completely. But it's still yours.

I wasn't discarding what had come before. I was claiming what was next.

And I trusted that whatever God was doing in me didn't need a map, only a willing yes.

So I gave it.

And everything that followed began to make sense.

What I Still Have to Give

There's a quiet kind of joy in reaching the highest point you ever wanted to reach, not the mountaintop everyone points to, but the one you chose for yourself. I got there. I stepped into the role I had always believed was mine to grow into. Not by chance, not by accident. I had earned every step. And I knew it.

It was the job I had dreamed of since finishing high school. It fit me down to the bone, technical, thoughtful, purpose-aligned. I was finally doing the work I was built to do, surrounded by peers who respected me, in a position that called on the full range of what I could offer.

I received the highest honors given at our agency for effort and contribution. Not because I asked for them. Because I lived them.

And when the time came to consider what came next, I didn't hesitate. I trained others. I handed down what I'd learned. I made sure someone else could pick up where I left off. I didn't want to hold on just because I could. I knew what staying too long looked like. I wasn't interested in decline. I was interested in release.

Contribution, to me, meant knowing when to carry and when to let go.

There was a time when I believed success had to be visible. I looked at the job titles, the awards, the quick promotions, and assumed those were the clearest signs someone had done something right.

But that changed.

Over the years, I noticed something else. People would stop me to mention a decision I barely remembered making, a comment I hadn't realized landed. It wasn't the formal achievements that stayed with them. It was the way I had shown up in a specific moment, calm, honest, steady.

At first, I didn't know that counted. Earlier in my career, I was still learning how to name it. Still figuring out what counted. I measured myself against pace and visibility. I watched others rise quickly, get noticed, move ahead. I tried to mimic the parts of them that got attention, confidence, polish, certainty, even when they didn't come naturally. I spent a long time wondering if my pace was a flaw.

It wasn't.

I was never lost. I was learning how to stay grounded.

Some people are meant to blaze through. Others are meant to steady the room. My contribution wasn't performance. It was presence. I stayed when others flinched. I paid attention to the things others overlooked. I wasn't trying to stand out, but I couldn't help seeing where something was off. Over time, that kind of attention started to matter.

The people I worked with didn't just improve technically, they grew more confident in their own judgment. I helped shape the policies, yes, but what mattered most to me was whether they held up in real situations. Whether they served the people they were written for.

I didn't take up a lot of space in meetings. That wasn't my way. But over time, folks came to rely on me. I listened closely. I paid attention. I was consistent, and that was enough.

In Romans 12, Paul reminds us: *"We have different gifts, according to the grace given to each of us"* (Romans 12:6, NIV). He doesn't rank them. He names them. The teacher. The encourager. The servant. Each essential. Each honored. Comparison tells us we have to stand out. Calling teaches us to stand firm in what is ours to do.

It's easy to forget that in a culture that rewards spectacle. We've been taught to equate visibility with value. But God has never measured worth that way.

Contribution, in God's economy, is about faithfulness. It's about showing up with what you have and offering it fully, not because it will go viral, but because it is true.

There came a moment in my final stretch, before retirement, before the handoff, when I knew I had done what I came to do. Not everything that could be done. But everything that was mine to carry.

I had reached the role I had envisioned. I had left nothing in reserve. And I had kept my integrity intact. Not because I clung tightly, but because I was willing to let go at the right time.

I wasn't chasing another rung. I was cultivating readiness, for someone else to rise.

When you stop chasing visibility, you begin to value what endures.

Impact isn't always dramatic. Sometimes it shows up as the person others trust in crisis. Sometimes it's the policy that protects someone you'll never meet. Sometimes it's the way your presence gives someone else permission to exhale.

We rarely talk about contribution in those terms. But that's what legacy actually looks like.

I've stopped asking, "Was I impressive?"

Now I ask, "Was I trustworthy?"

Because when your calling matures, the impulse to prove fades. What rises instead is the desire to give what's yours to give, and to step aside with grace when that work is complete.

At midlife and beyond, the questions shift:

- Am I still trying to impress people whose path I wouldn't want for myself?
- Am I honoring the season I'm in?
- Am I preparing others to carry what I once carried?

I've found a steadier rhythm lately, not because I have all the answers, but because I've stopped trying to adjust them for every new demand. I don't feel pulled in so many directions anymore. There's less urgency. More presence.

I'm not looking to be seen a certain way. I just want to be honest about what still belongs to me, and what I've outgrown.

At this point in the journey, I'm not leaving to be celebrated. I'm leaving because I know I've done what I came to do. The work mattered to me, and I stayed with it long enough to see it through. Not perfectly. But honestly.

That's what I think legacy really is. Not something loud. Not something polished. Just something true that holds, even when no one else is looking.

In the end, I don't need an audience.

I just want to leave knowing I lived like it mattered.

Chapter Six

When the Mirror Shifts

The Midlife Undoing

My 40's carried both faithfulness and fracture. We raised our daughter through ordinary storms, work, moves, unspoken disappointments. Commitment held us, but silence grew heavier than conversation, and distance steadier than devotion. By the time my daughter was fifteen, I knew I could not stay. I had left once before, briefly, during pregnancy, but returned. This time was different. This time I didn't come back. At forty-three, I walked away for good, carrying both grief and relief. It began with clarity.

The way I carried my life no longer matched the life I wanted.

Everything still functioned. My mind was sharp. My faith was strong. I knew who I was. But the structures I'd once relied on, identity, obligation, role, had started to loosen. And I had no desire to fasten them back in place.

The years that followed were not defined by another marriage, but by solitude. For the first seven, I gave myself to one of the most meaningful relationships of my life. When it ended, autumn after autumn brought a spiral I could almost time by the calendar. For three and a half years, depression overtook me each fall. Slowly, I began to climb out. I tried things I had never done before: hiking, weekly dances, wild caving, running 5Ks, showing up to renaissance fairs and group meals. I made friends, found new rhythms, and began to know myself outside of what anyone else required. By my mid-fifties, I had a niche, a steady circle, and the realization that I might one day want to share life again. Not out of desperation, but from steadiness.

Alongside that personal unfolding, I was mastering my craft. For fifteen years I worked in IT, deepening my expertise until I was known not only for survival, but for skill. It was a season of building authority, not from performance alone, but from resilience.

I'd spent decades being precise. Capable. Composed. I could hold a room without showing strain. I could make others feel at ease even when I was holding the hard edge of truth inside me. That was part of the training, family, work, church, all of it. Read the dynamics. Stay ahead of the disruption. Keep things on track.

That skill set had value. It got me through more than a few seasons that required it. But midlife brought a new kind of invitation, less about managing better, more about living differently.

I wasn't in crisis. I was clear. The performance was over.

Psychologists name this season "the second act transition", when the habits, identities, and measures of success from Act One begin to lose relevance. Robert Kegan calls it a move from "the socialized mind" to "the self-authoring mind." At some point, I stopped molding myself around the expectations I'd absorbed over the years. I began paying attention to what actually aligned with who I'd become, and letting the rest fall away.

This wasn't collapse. It was something more settled. A turn toward integrity.

I still showed up for my responsibilities, work, home, the people who counted on me. But I no longer made it my job to smooth every edge or manage other people's reactions. The contortion I used to call courtesy no longer served me.

My spiritual life stayed steady. My conversations with God deepened. I didn't ask for signs. I asked to stay in step with what He was already doing. The pruning didn't disturb me. It felt like precision.

John 15:2 kept echoing: *"Every branch that does bear fruit He prunes, that it may bear more fruit."* (ESV)

Clarity.

I wasn't losing anything essential.

I was returning to it.

Letting Go of Former Selves

Once things came into focus, I didn't wait around for someone to validate the shift. I didn't announce anything. I just started living differently.

My decisions came from a deeper place, from a steadiness that had been forming for a while. I wasn't trying to erase who I'd been. I just stopped letting old survival strategies take the lead.

It began with language. I stopped softening the truth to make it easier for others to hear. I brought forward what I saw, clean, sharp, accurate, and let it land. I didn't rush to explain. I didn't edit for comfort. That shift changed the tone of my presence almost immediately.

I also changed how I spent my time. I stopped saying yes out of obligation. I declined roles that no longer required my gifts, even when others assumed I'd say yes. I no longer measured my value by how much I could carry. I measured it by how much intention I brought to what I chose to carry.

In relationships, I stopped playing the translator. If someone didn't understand me, I let the misunderstanding stand. I no longer buffered my clarity with disclaimers. That wasn't defiance. It was stewardship. I had spent decades absorbing impact on behalf of others. Now, I was choosing how and when to engage, based not on need, but on trust.

These weren't dramatic acts. They were daily ones. I didn't reinvent myself. I moved with the version of me that had already emerged. The woman who knew how to think clearly, speak precisely, and discern what was hers to hold.

Some people faded out during that season. I hadn't turned cold, I just stopped overfunctioning in areas that no longer served me. The dynamic shifted, and the relationships that relied on me doing more than my share quietly dissolved. That loss made space for something sturdier.

My faith also changed shape. I no longer tried to fit a version of Christianity that rewarded silence and punished directness. I didn't feel the need to ask whether God approved of my boundaries. I had already asked the harder questions, and answered them with Scripture, prayer, and discernment. Romans 12:2 anchored me: *"Be transformed by the renewing of your mind."* That meant I could think differently. Live differently. Believe differently, without apology.

This, too, is individuation. It's integrating the parts of you that once fragmented to adapt come back together. Not in perfection, but in coherence.

That's what happened to me.

I stopped negotiating with my own wisdom. I started trusting it.

That trust changed how I moved. I stopped scattering my energy and started being deliberate, with my time, with my voice, with where I placed my attention. I didn't need recognition. I needed momentum. When something didn't align, I didn't force it.

Letting go of those older versions of myself wasn't nostalgia or grief. It was a shift in how I lived, rooted, steady, and wide awake to what mattered.

And from that clarity, I began building forward, one clean choice at a time.

Carrying Calling Through Resistance

It wasn't burnout in the way people describe, emotional collapse, total depletion, the need to disappear. I was still functioning. Still showing up. Still solving problems others couldn't see. Something had shifted, and I felt it before I could name it. The work itself hadn't changed, but what used to feel meaningful started to feel like a ceiling.

It wasn't the tasks that wore me down. It was the sense that I was being asked to play small in a space that no longer matched what I brought. I saw the gaps. I saw where things could be better. But there wasn't much appetite for that kind of clarity anymore. I had outgrown the shape of the role.

That discomfort didn't flatten me, it clarified me.

It showed me exactly what I had outlived: the need to stay small, the habit of deferring to gatekeepers, the assumption that being indispensable would one day be rewarded.

What I needed wasn't rest. It was redirection.

I had always seen the world through a systems lens. Long before the job titles or the training, I was tracking patterns, where the flow was interrupted, where the logic broke down, where unnecessary friction slowed things that should've worked. I didn't name it as strategy back then. I just knew how to make things run.

That instinct, the systems-mind I'd trusted all along, had already led me into the field where I finally found my fit. The pivot had come earlier, fast and focused, in the years when time was short and the stakes were high. I'd returned to school, earned the degree, stepped into the role. That story had already unfolded. What burnout revealed now was something different: the cost of staying aligned in a system that didn't always want to be examined.

When I entered the field, I didn't make noise. I made progress. I took on roles that fit how I thought. I offered solutions, kept learning, and let the work speak for itself. Over time, people started to recognize what I carried. I was doing the work well, and building credibility as I went.

That stretch, where the systems aligned with my thinking, where my insight was trusted and my influence respected, became the most grounded, satisfying season of my vocational life.

I wasn't just operating as an employee. I was operating as an analyst, an architect, a steward of structure. It comes through decades of quiet observation, through trusting what others overlooked, through refusing to settle for roles that only needed half of you.

Jesus said in Luke 16:10, *"Whoever is faithful in very little is also faithful in much."* For a long time, I stayed present in places that made very little room for what I carried. I solved problems inside systems that ran on dysfunction. I brought insight into roles that couldn't quite name it.

Even so, I kept showing up. And over time, that persistence shaped something deeper, discernment that could hold steady when the pressure rose.

By the time I reached the highest role I ever wanted, I didn't have anything to prove. I had already proven it, quietly, over time, through integrity, consistency, and a mind that refused to settle.

The quiet truth I now carried was that I had more to offer than some systems were willing to hold.

That pressed me to stop settling for work that only half fit. I began choosing roles that matched what I could actually offer. I led with more presence, less apology. I put my energy where it could build something real, and let go of the rest.

That choice made everything else possible.

Freedom in Limits

I used to think strength meant capacity, the ability to do more, hold more, stretch further. And for a long time, it did. I raised a daughter, worked full time, showed up in every room that asked something of me. That way of living built discipline. It shaped endurance. It made certain things possible.

But this stretch of life calls for something else: precision.

I no longer equate fullness with volume. I measure it by clarity: what fits, what fuels, what flows.

Every yes now carries more weight. Every no clears ground for something that matters more. I move deliberately because I learned to aim.

This is the season where purpose chooses its partners. I don't go everywhere I'm invited. I show up where my presence can carry something real. That applies to projects, friendships, decisions about how I spend a single afternoon. I value momentum, but I value stewardship more.

Vocationally, I still think in systems. I still find satisfaction in making something work better than it did before. But I no longer feel responsible for fixing every broken process, or every broken dynamic. I offer insight where it lands. I let the rest go. I know what's mine to carry, and what's not.

This kind of focus doesn't shrink life. It sharpens it. When you stop scattering your energy across every expectation, you start leaving a trail that actually points somewhere. That's what legacy is. Not a long list of titles. A clean arc of integrity.

In Exodus 18, Moses learns this lesson the hard way. He's exhausted, managing every dispute among the people, standing in the gap from dawn until dusk. His father-in-law, Jethro, watches for a while before stepping in. "*What you are doing is not good,*" he tells him. "*You will wear yourselves out... The work is too heavy for you; you cannot handle it alone.*" (Exodus 18:17–18, NIV)

Jethro wasn't criticizing Moses' effort. He was protecting his longevity.

That same principle guides me now. I make decisions not only based on ability, but on sustainability. Will this stretch of labor bring me deeper into what I'm here to do? Will it draw out my wisdom, my clarity, my presence? Or will it just drain my hours?

I don't perform usefulness anymore. I embody it, intentionally, selectively, with joy.

Even relationships require discernment. I no longer carry the emotional load for people unwilling to carry their own. I don't stretch to be understood. I speak clearly. I move on. That's not distance, it's discipline. It allows me to invest more fully in the relationships that give and receive truth.

Time isn't something I fill. It's something I hold open. For reflection. For service. For the quiet work of preparing what's next. I don't know how many years I have left. But I know how I want to spend them, offering what's mine to give, where it can do the most good.

This is what freedom looks like now.

A life shaped by intention, not interruption. A rhythm led by discernment, not demand. A legacy made visible, not in crowds or applause, but in the quiet clarity of a life well-aimed.

This stretch is no longer about proving strength.

It's about stewarding it wisely.

Chapter Seven

BECOMING AN ELDER-IN-TRAINING

Releasing the Role of Parent

By the time your child becomes an adult, you've already handed over more than you realize, meals, memories, instincts, fears, prayers. And if you've been doing the deeper work, you've also released control long before the last curfew lifts. You learn to lead with trust. You learn to surrender what you can't script.

Parenting ends differently than it begins. It starts loud and urgent, full of logistics and vigil. It ends quietly, if you let it. Not with a speech or a ceremony, but with a series of silent recognitions: this choice is hers to make. That opinion doesn't need to be shared. This conversation isn't mine to lead.

You never stop being a parent, but you do stop parenting. That's the pivot.

It's not abandonment. It's boundary. It's the sacred shift from director to witness.

You raised them to become. That was the point. Not to orbit you, not to mirror you, but to live. To follow the voice of God for themselves, not filtered through your convictions. When that begins to happen, you can either release with peace or resist with anxiety. The first path opens space for relationship. The second corrodes it.

This release isn't just about your child. It's about you. When the doing stops, the identity you built around it dissolves, and that's essential. Parenting, as a role, has a shelf life. Eldering does not. You're not exiting usefulness. You're reorienting it.

For me, that shift came gradually, then suddenly. My daughter had moved out, built a life of her own. We spoke often, but our dynamic changed. She came to me with questions, not dependence. She processed things aloud but decided without permission. And I felt it, deep in my spirit, this is the transition. I was no longer the authority. I was now the example. Not to be followed, but to be referenced. My job wasn't to guide her every step. I knew my job had changed. She didn't need my oversight, she needed a reference point. So I turned toward living my own life with integrity, trusting that if she ever looked over, she'd see faithfulness holding its shape.

Our love didn't fade. It sharpened. Once I stopped managing her needs, the space between us got cleaner. Less tied to obligation. More grounded in truth. I didn't have to walk beside her to stay connected. I stood where I was, steady, and let her go where she needed to go.

Of course, there's grief in the shift, especially if your identity was overly fused with motherhood. The empty space feels foreign at first. But it's not a loss. It's a return. You were someone before they arrived. You remain someone still.

Some parents struggle to let go because they never got to live out their own story fully. They attach meaning to their child's choices, hoping to redeem something in themselves. That's not love. That's longing in disguise. When you release the role, you also free your child from carrying your unfulfilled hopes. You get to reclaim what was buried, not to make up for the past, but to steward what's still ahead.

Scripture affirms this rhythm of release. Abraham let go of Isaac. Hannah gave Samuel back to God. Mary stepped aside as Jesus stepped into ministry. At every key threshold, a parent steps back, not because they've stopped loving, but because they've loved well. Autonomy is not rebellion. It's the fruit of obedience, to your calling and theirs.

Even Jesus, in His final moments, honored His mother without clinging to her. He entrusted her care to another disciple as completion. His role as son was not His identity. He knew when the shift had come.

We would do well to learn that same timing.

The transition also invites forgiveness, yours and theirs. You'll remember mistakes. They will too. But elderhood doesn't require perfection. It requires honesty. When you own what's yours without collapse or defense, you model spiritual maturity. You say: "This was mine to carry, and I carry it still, but I won't let it define me, or us."

This is where relationship often deepens. Without the parent-child hierarchy, you meet each other again, adult to adult, soul to soul. You laugh differently. You listen more. You stop measuring your success by their choices. You start respecting their process.

You begin to see them with cleaner eyes. And they begin to see you as more than a title.

This is how love matures.

Parenting was never meant to be permanent. Stewardship always has a handoff. And if you've done your work, you don't step away in regret. You step aside with peace.

And in that space, a new role begins to take shape, not as parent, but as elder-in-training. Someone who no longer holds the rope, but who knows where to stand as others begin their climb.

Individuating Again in Later Adulthood

Individuation isn't a single act. It's a pattern. It returns every time you outgrow an identity that once defined you. For some, it first arrives in adolescence. For others, in early adulthood. But it resurfaces later too, when the roles that shaped you start to release their grip.

Later adulthood brings a kind of liberation that rarely gets acknowledged. After you've raised a child, buried a parent, carried your share of burden, something else begins to surface. The striving slows. What remains is quieter, but clearer. You start recognizing your essence, the self that doesn't need to prove anything to exist.

You're staying rooted. Just no longer running on autopilot. The role served its season, now it's time to serve from truth. Precision takes the place of performance. You stop trying to become someone and start honoring who's been there all along, beneath the survival strategies, beneath the persona.

For many women, the role of mother becomes a container for identity. For men, it may be provider, achiever, protector. There's no shame in those roles, but they grow rigid if never examined.

When the demands of work and family begin to fade, something else comes into view. What was always underneath. And whether you welcome it or resist it, it rises.

The questions change. You no longer ask, "What do I need to do?" You ask, "What do I want to keep doing?" "What still feels honest?" You start to choose based on resonance rather than recognition. On alignment, not obligation.

That isn't selfishness. It's maturity. You're no longer defining yourself through sacrifice. You're clarifying who and what you were entrusted to steward, starting with your own soul. This is refinement, not departure. A convergence of your lived experience and original design.

Jung called it shadow integration. In practice, it feels like pruning. You stop tolerating what flattens you. You stop justifying choices that cost more than they return. You don't have to explain. You just begin to live more cleanly.

This is often a season of reclamation. Creativity returns, but not as performance. Solitude becomes useful again. The pace slows, by choice, not decline. You stop needing to prove you can keep up, and start paying attention to what's actually worth carrying forward. There's strength in that shift. Not the kind that strives, but the kind that holds.

In my own life, I stopped explaining myself. I quit doing favors I didn't want to do. I backed out of spaces that drained me. The people who stayed belonged. The ones who left made space. That was the shift. No drama, just done.

And it matters, spiritually. Elderhood isn't about legacy. It's about alignment. You don't drift into wisdom. You return to it, through Scripture, through prayer, through moments when the Spirit speaks in subtleties.

In your younger years, you differentiated to find yourself. Now, you differentiate to stay honest. You begin to notice when old strategies expire. And you don't panic. You release them, knowing that letting go is part of formation.

Sometimes that means revisiting friendships. Sometimes it means admitting you no longer enjoy the life you built. Sometimes it means telling the truth out loud for the first time.

It doesn't require fanfare. Just permission.

This isn't rebellion. It's reordering.

You already know you are loved. You've already been seen by the only One who matters. What follows isn't performance. It's offering.

This is the bridge between survival and service. You stop managing your image. You start cultivating your influence. Not because time is short, but because now, it's finally yours.

And from this place, you begin to mentor. That doesn't mean shaping others into your image, but affirming the shape they're already becoming. Individuation doesn't end with self-discovery. It extends into witness. It moves from clarity to offering. And from offering to presence.

You stop holding your truth.

You start embodying it.

The Gift of Perspective

With age, your vantage point changes. You're no longer in the trenches of immediacy. The urgent becomes less compelling. The personal reveals itself as pattern. You begin to see with greater distance, and that distance brings clarity.

Perspective isn't guaranteed. Some grow older clinging to injury, identity, or control. But if you're willing to release the stories that once framed your worth, you begin to see differently. You stop narrating from the center of pain. You step to the edge and look with steadiness. The facts remain, but the fear no longer narrates them.

This isn't detachment. It's discernment. Indifference hardens the heart. Perspective softens it. You feel compassion for people you once resented. You understand decisions that once baffled you. You lose the appetite for proving your point. You carry your convictions without trying to convert. That's where wisdom begins.

Time reveals patterns. You see how seasons loop. How certain outcomes take decades. You recognize seeds when they're planted, even if the harvest will outlive you. You stop insisting on immediacy. You stop demanding resolution. Some fruit ripens slowly, and some will never be yours to taste. That no longer bothers you.

This clarity is spiritual. Proverbs names gray hair a crown of glory. Aging itself isn't what is sacred, but it makes space for truth. In Christ, wisdom is not information, it's humility lived out. The longer you walk with God, the more you understand your need for grace. You posture less. You pretend less. You listen more.

In youth, strength looks like certainty. In elderhood, it looks like mercy.

Perspective also reorders your energy. You stop pouring yourself into every crisis. You learn the difference between urgency and calling. Not every comment needs a response. Not every tension needs resolution. You start responding from your core, not your reflex. That shift doesn't make you passive. It makes you powerful in quieter ways.

Elders know what to speak, and when silence holds more. They speak from weight, not volume. They don't rush clarity. They let it arrive.

Perspective also allows for paradox. You no longer need things to resolve on your timeline. You can hold opposing truths at once. You can love someone you disagree with. You can forgive someone who will never apologize. You no longer demand life to be fair, you trust it to be meaningful.

This doesn't come from avoidance. It comes from pattern recognition. From watching long enough to recognize God's fingerprints in the very places you once named chaos.

The outcomes still matter. You just care differently. You hold your influence loosely. What is yours to carry will stay. What is not can be released. This is where true authority begins, in presence.

There's a kind of forgiveness that only perspective makes possible. You stop requiring apologies to move forward. You stop identifying with your injuries. You see more fully now, how limited some people's tools were. It doesn't erase what happened. It just loosens your tether to it. The scar remains. The sting does not.

You start to see yourself differently, too. The failures that once haunted you now feel instructive. You don't romanticize them, but you don't let them own you either. You no longer perform redemption. You live it.

Your worth stops riding on productivity. Your value anchors in fruitfulness, love, clarity, peace, courage. You care more about who you are becoming than what you are building. This is where legacy begins, not with what you leave behind, but with what you carry faithfully while you're still here.

Perspective reshapes everything. It changes how you show up in rooms, how you parent your adult children, how you spend your remaining hours. It becomes a filter. A guide. A center.

And it's something you can give. Not through advice. Through example. Your presence becomes steady enough to shelter others.

Your words don't instruct, they illuminate. People seek you out for the groundedness you carry.

That's the mark of an elder-in-training: clarity without noise. Presence without performance.

You see differently now, steady, reverent, aligned.

You see the long arc of healing.

You see process as sacred.

You see the slow work of God, still unfolding.

Preparing to Be Poured Out

There comes a moment in later adulthood when the current shifts. The energy that once went into building, striving, accumulating, now begins to move outward. No agenda. No saving. You're handing off what's no longer yours to hold.

You begin to give from a place of fullness. From a life examined, tested, held. You no longer need to curate what you've learned. You just make it available. Without polish. Without performance.

This is the posture of elderhood: to pour out without depletion, to offer without attachment, to speak without control.

Paul, nearing the end of his life, wrote: *"I am already being poured out like a drink offering."* He didn't resist it. He had lived what he was given. Now he was releasing it.

That kind of surrender doesn't come overnight. It takes work. The parts of your life you haven't faced will block the flow. What's unresolved stays stuck. If you want to be poured out, you have to take your life seriously. Sort it. Name it. Let God shape it into something someone else can use.

This is where your weight begins to shift. You're no longer in motion just to stay moving. What you carry now is distilled. You don't give out of pressure. You give because something in you is ready.

Not everything will land. Some moments will pass unnoticed. That doesn't change what you've offered.

You're not building anything new. You're releasing what God gave you to carry while you still have the strength to carry it well.

That's the paradox: the looser your grip, the more people trust what you carry. They sense the absence of agenda. They feel the authority of a life no longer performing. You don't have to convince anyone. You've already lived it.

Being poured out isn't about burnout. It's about alignment. You give what is yours to give. You say what needs to be said. You serve not because you have to, but because you can. Because you've been shaped by something deeper than ambition. Because you've been held through more than one kind of storm.

And in this posture, your own preparation continues. You begin to hold less. You spend more carefully. You give your time and attention without trying to steer the outcome. Your story is no longer a tool, it's simply available. You don't need to speak to make something real. Presence carries its own weight.

You move through the day with less grip. What comes in, you hold. What's ready, you give. No scorekeeping. No strategy. Just steady alignment with the One who gave it in the first place.

This is the quiet distinction of an elder-in-training: the life no longer points inward. It points to the Source. It isn't a monument. It's a current. The words don't declare. They confirm.

There's no need to be remembered. The aim is to be faithful.

And in that faithfulness, what's been carried is handed off, open-handed, unguarded, whole.

Because it was never theirs to keep.

Act III: Blessing

The Act of Offering

Chapter Eight

The Gift of Redirection

Retiring the Résumé

The shift had already happened by the time I noticed it.

I was halfway through my coffee, driving to my part-time job at the pharmacy, when my eyes landed on the old parking permit still resting on the dash. It had been there for months, maybe longer, but I'd never really seen it. Not like that.

It didn't feel current anymore. I suppose some part of me felt it still had something to say. It reminded me of the long stretch I'd spent building a life of structure, professional, dependable, rooted in decades of steady labor. A season of leadership, advocacy, promotion, and presence. That version of me wore the title well. Her role mattered. Her decisions had weight. She stepped aside when it was time, quietly, without needing applause.

I can still see her clearly. She served her purpose, fully and well. But someone else is driving now.

That moment in the car didn't feel nostalgic. Just honest. Something in me had already shifted. I parked, walked into the pharmacy, and slid behind the front counter like I'd always belonged there. Patients began to trickle in, each one familiar, each one with a story I've come to know. Some bring their grief in their posture. Some bring their joy in their voices. All of them bring something real. And I get to meet them where they are.

This is work I absolutely love. Local. Relational. Consistent. I arrive ready to serve, to bring my best attention, to offer what's needed in that hour and no more. No ladder to climb. No performance to refine. Just the daily practice of being dependable in a place where dependability matters.

That old résumé, tucked away in a drawer at home, tells a true story. It reflects perseverance, systems thinking, creative problem-solving, hard-earned leadership. It earned me a place at tables where decisions were made. It helped me raise my daughter, provide for my family, and steward the kind of legacy that leaves quiet echoes in its wake. Its time was full.

And its season is complete.

Psychologist Helen Rose Fuchs Ebaugh named this transition "role exit", the movement that unfolds when long-held identities release their shape. Not because the person has vanished, but because the scaffolding no longer fits. What rises next is not a question of reinvention. It's a question of continuity.

Who am I, now that the roles have changed?

The answer comes gently. I am a woman who welcomes the people in front of her. Who remembers their names. Who makes space for others to feel safe in their own skin. The capacities I spent a career developing didn't dissolve. They redirected.

The kingdom of God has always honored that kind of redirection. When God invited Moses to lead, He didn't list his credentials. He pointed to what was already in his hand. (Exodus 4:2). The assignment wasn't earned. It was entrusted. And the answer that mattered wasn't a résumé. It was willingness.

What's in my hand now?

A smile. A steady tone. A patient's sigh of relief when I say, "It's so good to see you again!"

At home, I've found a similar rhythm. My new marriage, four years in, continues to teach me the holy labor of mutual growth. We weather storms, raised voices, difficult family dynamics, each of us sorting through our own edges until calm returns. There were seasons with addiction in the house, extended family folding into our space, and chaos pressing in. But we're learning how to hold the line together. We practice steadiness. We choose to remain.

The atmosphere is different. Grounded. Honest. We don't reach for perfection. We reach for self-awareness. And that, too, is a kind of offering.

I no longer feel responsible for every detail of everyone's experience. I no longer carry other people's tension as my own. I walk into rooms with open eyes, ready to be present but not absorbed. That shift didn't come from burnout or crisis. It came from maturing. It came from choosing peace as a practice rather than a reward.

The résumé version of my life was never a performance. It was real. It built something worthy. But it no longer holds the center.

Now, the center belongs to presence. Presence in the lives of those I serve at the pharmacy. Presence in my home, where peace is protected without being forced. Presence in my own body, where age has softened urgency and made space for steadier forms of joy.

The résumé stays in the drawer. It has done its work. It no longer guides my days. I remain engaged, useful, delighted to contribute.

But contribution looks different now. It doesn't arrive as effort. It arrives as alignment.

God continues to make use of what I carry.

And I continue to offer it, freely, from the center of who I am.

Becoming Useful in New Ways

Over time, a different kind of usefulness began to rise.

After years of structured output, projects completed, problems solved, people guided, I noticed something else emerging. Discernment. Attunement. The ability to sense what mattered before it was spoken. These weren't new capacities. They had simply waited for the right season.

This is that season.

Now, usefulness flows through presence. Through steadiness. Sometimes it's as simple as staying put when the room feels unsure.

Meaning shows up in strange ways. A neighbor starts talking about the weather but can't seem to stop. Someone behind me at the store drops a single sentence that hangs there, unguarded, unfinished. A message comes in from a friend who doesn't need anything specific, just wants to be less alone for a minute.

These aren't detours. They're thresholds. Brief chances to meet someone in the middle of their day, exactly as they are.

Earlier in life, value often showed up as momentum. I worked hard. I solved problems. I built systems that held. That work mattered, and I gave it everything I had.

Now the questions have changed again.

What deserves care?

What can I hold with gentleness?

What wisdom belongs here, in this moment, for this person?

At the pharmacy, I'm often asked to train new hires. My supervisor values the patience and thoroughness I bring to the process, offering details others might not think to include. I've always had a mind for what makes things work. That's still true. I'll step in, simplify the process, walk through it side by side. At times, I'll catch the rhythm of my own approach echoing through the room, another colleague greeting a patient the way I had, using a tone or gesture that feels familiar. And I'll smile.

That small echo feels like joy.

I only recently came across the term generativity, coined by developmental psychologist Erik Erikson. It describes a life stage marked by contribution rather than accumulation, by the desire to nourish what's still unfolding and to offer what's been gathered. Of course there was already a word for that, but the practice had already begun.

That's what usefulness looks like now.

No urgency. No ladder to climb. Just the steady rhythm of contributing what still lives in the hand.

Sometimes it's a story that lands at just the right moment.

Other times, it's the steady quiet between words, the kind that doesn't need a reason.

Even a look can carry something whole: I see you. I'm not going anywhere.

That kind of usefulness doesn't need a title. It lives in the body. It holds.

Leaving Roles, Returning Whole

The roles we carry often begin as callings. Over time, they become identities. Eventually, they ask to be released.

Retirement made that clear. The shift arrived gradually but decisively, like handing in a key that once opened everything. I had lived for years inside roles that gave shape and direction: worker, advocate, provider, manager. Each asked something real of me. Each offered meaning in return. And I brought my full self to them.

Eventually, it was time to lay them down.

Ebaugh's idea of role exit goes beyond a change in schedule; it marks a departure that reshapes your sense of self. When a long-held identity begins to fade, something new stirs beneath it. That in-between place can feel hard to name. There's no map for it. But it hums with possibility.

That's where I found myself, quiet enough, finally, to start listening.

The daily scripts had gone quiet. What remained was something deeper. The roles I had held weren't burdens, they were scaffolding. They supported growth, revealed strength, carried me through loss and purpose and effort. But over time, scaffolding gives way to structure. And the soul asks for more rooted ground.

Scripture names this kind of threshold. In Luke 2, we meet the prophetess Anna, widowed for decades, faithful in her temple service. Her story spans only a few verses, yet God places her at the moment of Christ's dedication. She speaks blessing over the Messiah before many understand who He is. Her presence doesn't resume an old role. It radiates from the center of a life formed in devotion.

That's what sacred reentry looks like.

Sacred reentry begins when value no longer flows through visibility. When presence stands in for performance. When the soul steps forward, not with ambition, but with attention.

The body offers cues for this transition. Energy settles into a slower current. Sleep deepens. Urgency loosens its grip. The nervous system learns to trust that the proving season has passed. And yet, meaning still pulses underneath.

Meaning now lives in participation. In alignment. In small acts of presence that feel whole even without explanation.

This reentry doesn't require a new role. It welcomes a new posture.

Tasks lost their pull. What held my attention instead were the quiet things: a conversation without hurry, the way late light stretched across the table. I began to notice moments I used to skim past, a glance that steadied the room, a pause that allowed itself to remain, presence that didn't need to declare itself.

There's something steady in this season. Room to linger. Room to respond gently, instead of quickly. Grace to move gently when others press forward.

Carl Jung believed that later adulthood brings the soul's essential material to the surface, dreams that clarify, questions that expand, truths that gather toward the center.

Reentry becomes sacred when the question shifts from *What should I do now?* to *How can I embody what I've come to know?*

That question drew me into new rhythms, some social, some solitary. I reentered my own story without needing to rewrite it. I began writing books in my 60s, first as protest, then as pattern. Some were born of frustration, some from moral clarity, and others from the kind of quiet wonder that comes when a subject catches hold of my mind and doesn't let go. The work changed. The context changed. But the core remained.

I still show up. Still offer help when asked. Still carry wisdom forward, not as expertise, but as offering.

Now and then, someone asks what I "do" now. I could give a list, part-time responsibilities, occasional projects, ways I stay engaged. But the truest answer lives beneath all that:

I remain awake.

I remain available.

I remain attuned to the sacred that still stirs, even when no one is keeping score.

Sacred reentry doesn't need a platform. It asks for readiness.

This third movement unfolds without spectacle. There's no reinvention here, only a quieter, deeper continuation. I bring what I carry. I offer what remains true. And I trust that God, who shaped every earlier role, continues to shape this one as well.

This is reentry born of blessing.

This is usefulness anchored in presence.

This is life, once again, becoming whole.

Joy Without Credentials

Some joys arrive without invitation. Others begin to bloom when invitation is no longer required.

In this season, joy moves differently. It flows beneath the surface, steady, unforced, fully alive.

Earlier in life, joy often followed achievement. Effort led to recognition. Contribution created momentum. Being chosen, praised, or trusted opened doors that shaped identity. Those moments mattered. They built something solid.

But now, joy rises from a quieter place. It asks for nothing in return.

Joy in the way morning light settles across the floorboards.

Joy in the hum of a song I didn't realize I'd been singing.

Joy in music chosen by instinct, no memory attached, just rhythm, just melody, just breath.

These joys arrive not through striving, but through presence.

Joy, as Scripture frames it, isn't something to chase. It takes root in connection. In John 15:11, Jesus says, *"I have told you this so that my joy may be in you and that your joy may be complete."* He's pointing toward love that holds, remaining in Him, staying close to others, living grounded in what endures. The image of the vine helps me see it clearly: joy doesn't come from striving. It comes from staying.

That truth has stayed with me.

Joy flows through alignment now, through awareness, through attention, through being fully present to the goodness already here. It lives in simplicity, in rhythm, in the ordinary sacred of a well-lived day.

For years, joy wore the garments of productivity. Now it wears something softer.

I find joy in sitting beside someone, even when words stay quiet.

I find joy in sharing what I carry, even when the world leans toward spectacle.

I find joy in rest that holds no requirement, just the breath returning to itself.

Psychologists call this intrinsic fulfillment. Abraham Maslow, later in life, spoke of "being values": truth, simplicity, beauty, wholeness. These aren't achieved. Joy doesn't always explain itself. Sometimes it's just there, familiar, quiet, easy to miss. I notice it more often now: on a walk, in a slow conversation, in the space between doing and undoing. It doesn't need to be claimed or earned. It just settles in, reminding me I haven't missed a thing.

No credentials make it stronger. No title makes it true. No stage needed. It lives in the marrow. It lives in the ease that arrives when life and soul begin to move in rhythm.

Each morning, I wake without any agenda to impress. And still, joy meets me.

It meets me in the way my husband sets my coffee cup exactly where I like it.

It meets me in a message from someone long ago, thanking me for a kindness I'd forgotten I gave.

It meets me in the song I choose to sing, not for performance, but because the voice inside me feels full.

Joy rests in being.

And from that place of being, new offerings rise, freely, quietly, without calculation. Not as obligation, but as overflow.

There's joy in feeling useful. And equal joy in choosing simplicity.

There's joy in being asked. And joy, too, in being ready when no one asks.

Joy no longer waits for conditions to be right. It walks beside me now, steady and sacred.

Credentials shaped earlier seasons. They opened doors, lent authority, built trust. But the soul carries its own authority once it begins to live from wisdom. From peace. From grace.

This is joy redefined.

It asks for no audience. It reflects no résumé.

It lingers. It steadies.

It glows.

Chapter Nine

Letting Light Spill

Becoming a Blessing, Not a Brand

My life holds fewer definitions now. I move through the world with ease shaped by years, not urgency. There's no effort to explain who I am or to signal something beyond what's true in the moment. I know how to show up, and I trust what arrives through that alone.

The pharmacy grounds me in this rhythm. Most people there don't know what I used to do. They know the way I greet them. They know I pay attention. They recognize something steady and familiar in how I move through the day. That's enough. The exchanges are often brief, but they carry weight. I catch what's unspoken. I meet people where they are, not where they feel expected to be.

Years ago, I shaped myself to meet the room. I could read a room before I even stepped into it. Years of necessity shaped that instinct, I knew how to track tone, energy, the undercurrent of what wasn't being said. I offered what seemed needed, often before anyone asked. That kept me safe. It also earned respect. People counted on me to steady things. And I did. But over time, I felt the cost. I gave more than I had. I started anticipating reactions I hadn't even received. I held steady, but not without cost. The questions didn't disappear, they just dropped out of sight. I stayed composed, or at least looked it. But composure can run parallel to depletion. I shaped a version of myself that worked, dependable, contained, easier for others to understand. It wasn't a lie. It just wasn't the whole story. I knew what to bring forward. I knew what to withhold.

Back then, I framed it as discernment. With distance, I recognize it for what it was, adaptation. Necessary, maybe, but draining. That's how the shaping begins. Not with deception, but with small edits. What started as clarity turns into presentation. Usefulness shifts into performance. Over time, the version you've built becomes heavier to carry. You hear yourself hesitate in places where honesty once came easily. You sense the gap between what you feel and what you're willing to say out loud. You learn how to survive without revealing too much. It works until it wears out.

Blessing asks for something different. It moves through presence, not polish. It enters slowly and waits to be received. There's no formula. No script. Just a way of being that clears space for someone else to feel whole again.

Two months before I stepped away from career, I entered a second marriage. Retirement and remarriage arrived almost hand-in-hand, opening a season that asked new things of me: steadiness, honesty, and shared resilience through storms neither of us expected. Six months after retirement, I found myself back at work, part-time in a local store. A year later, I trained as a Pharmacy

Technician, a role I still hold. It was not the career I once pursued with ambition, but a way to stay present, useful, and connected.

Scripture calls us to be light. *"Let your light shine before others,"* Jesus said, *"that they may see your good deeds and glorify your Father in heaven"* (Matthew 5:16). That kind of light doesn't perform. It doesn't seek applause. It reveals what's already sacred.

The more I've lived, the more I've let that be enough. I don't prepare my life to be impressive. I prepare it to be useful. I carry what I've learned into every room, sometimes through words, sometimes just by listening longer than most people will.

Rogers' words still held: *"When I accept myself just as I am, then I can change."* It was true in the unraveling of youth, and it was just as true here, in later years, as acceptance ripened into offering. Acceptance, to me, feels less like a pivot point and more like a resting place. I stopped adjusting. I stopped scanning the room for cues. That space once filled with evaluation now holds peace.

Writing entered during this same season. I began putting words on paper because something in me asked to be spoken. I've always written with the hope of being useful. That question, who will this reach?, shapes the tone, the depth, the form. It doesn't steer the truth, but it helps the truth land.

These pages are themselves the fruit of that decision. Writing became my offering, the way to gather up decades of becoming and building, and hand them back to the wider community. Not as authority, but as witness. As grace carried forward.

That same posture lives in how I move through the day. My voice has changed. My timing has changed. There's less urgency. More alignment. I speak when prompted, leave space when that feels better, and let the silence stretch longer than I once could have tolerated.

There's no need to be memorable. I'd rather be steady. People carry their own burdens. I don't need to add complexity. I aim to bring peace, clarity, a little warmth. That feels like wholeness, earned, not announced.

Legacy, from this vantage point, doesn't cling to artifacts. It shows up in subtler ways. A line someone repeats without knowing where they heard it. A conversation that left the air gentler than it was before. A room that felt less sharp because of how you entered it. My husband has a phrase he uses when he's teaching his daughters how to live well in the world: *"People won't remember what you said. They remember how you made them feel."* He's right. You can leave a lasting mark without leaving your name. These are the echoes that stay. They don't depend on being noticed to leave their mark.

We're taught to make ourselves visible. To craft a self that can be named, explained, remembered. Faith teaches something simpler, walk with integrity. Speak with care. Let what's inside match what's offered. Create space for God to move through what remains.

I choose that.

Each time.

What Leaves a Trace

Influence used to come through roles, some formal, some absorbed by necessity.

Lead, operator, analyst, technician. Those were the titles on paper.

Parent, mentor, manager, subject matter expert, those emerged in the gaps, wherever steadiness or clarity was needed and someone had to carry it.

I took those roles seriously. They weren't ceremonial. People entrusted me with more than tasks. They looked to me for steadiness, and I understood what that required. I got better at listening beneath the surface, at recognizing the moment to act, and the moment to hold. The work matured me. What I once thought was about guidance became something quieter. Less instruction, more presence.

As for the people who influenced me, none were permanent. They passed through a chapter or two, offered something true, then moved on. What they gave stayed longer than they did. A few friends moved through meaningful chapters with me. We shared moments of clarity, grief, growth. Sometimes just a conversation that stayed lodged in memory long after the person moved on. They didn't guide my life. But during the time we walked together, they helped me see a little more clearly.

Those moments mattered.

Not because they provided what I lacked, but because they made room for what I carried.

Mentorship shows up that way more often than people admit. Quiet. Unscheduled. Shaped by trust more than instruction.

I've mentored in structured settings and informal ones, through work, through relationships, through conversations that started as something else entirely. The moments that linger didn't begin with announcements. They came through side doors. A comment in a hallway. A glance across a table. A story shared during a long drive. You don't always know when the moment is happening. You just feel the stillness it leaves behind.

Creativity carries that same shape. In younger years, the work reached for affirmation. The goal was clarity, polish, impact. That made sense for the time. It built skill. But something shifted later. The work started asking for more truth and less performance.

The energy behind it felt different, less about display, more about integrity.

In this stage of life, mentoring and creativity feel intertwined. Both move through presence. Both ask for attention over control. I speak when prompted. I hold back when the moment asks for space. I offer questions more often than answers.

The invitation now is to walk alongside, not to direct.

Psychologist Daniel Siegel describes "mindsight" as the ability to perceive another person's interior state while remaining anchored in your own. That's the shape of influence I trust most, attentive but grounded. Present without absorbing. Steady without trying to solve.

Mentorship becomes sacred when it honors someone's unfolding without inserting your own shape over theirs.

Creative work becomes sacred when it reflects reality instead of performance.

Influence comes quietly now. No invitations. No fanfare. I notice when someone watches how I handle a situation, then adjusts their own approach. I hear my phrasing echoed later in another conversation. I sense a shift when I stay calm during tension, and someone else steadies themselves in response. No one names it, but something moves. A mood recalibrates. A choice becomes easier. That's how influence travels here, through example more than exchange.

Scripture holds example after example of this kind of influence.

Elizabeth greets Mary not with advice, but recognition. Naomi walks with Ruth through grief and transition. Barnabas steps into Paul's story at the moment others are still unsure what to make of him. These weren't performances. These were steady acts of presence that helped others become more fully themselves.

Jesus lived this rhythm every day. He moved slowly enough to be interrupted. He asked questions without rushing toward resolution. He taught through proximity, not position. People felt seen in His presence, long before they felt instructed.

When I write now, the energy comes from that same place. I think about the person reading quietly on a morning they didn't know would carry a shift. I don't write to be remembered. I write to offer what's been given to me in a way that can travel.

Real influence doesn't require recognition. It just asks for alignment.

I think of the people who once walked beside me for a season. Their presence steadied something. Their words stayed with me. They never claimed authority. They simply offered care in real time. That's the shape my own mentoring takes now. No program. No performance. Just presence.

I don't try to create impact anymore. I pay attention. When something calls to be said, I say it. When the moment feels too tender for advice, I stay quiet. When someone falters, I don't rush to fix. I stay close.

Influence works that way. Steady. Quiet. Honest.

And it does its best work when no one's tracking it.

The Spiritual Discipline of Showing Up

Some of the most sacred acts in my life have taken place without fanfare.

Being where I said I'd be. Staying longer than expected. Returning when I could have walked away. This wasn't because I had the answer, but because something in me knew the moment required presence more than intervention.

That's what I mean by showing up. A discipline of being available without performance. Attention without demand. Presence that steadies rather than explains.

In a culture that rewards strategy and spectacle, real presence resets the pace. It alters the emotional temperature in a room. It allows truth to rise instead of being pulled.

There are plenty of ways to define spiritual maturity: doctrine, insight, mystical experience, but I've come to recognize it most clearly in those who remain. Not out of obligation. Out of alignment.

God's story unfolds through presence. Burning bush. Desert silence. Flesh and blood. Incarnation was never abstract. *"God with us"* wasn't a symbol, it was a claim on time, space, body. And now, the charge is ours to carry that presence forward.

When the Holy Spirit enters, it doesn't overtake. It settles. And from that stillness, action follows.

Early on, I misunderstood presence as something to fill. I thought I needed to bring comfort, perspective, insight. Now I see it differently. Sometimes what's most needed isn't a solution, but your steadiness. Silence can hold as much weight as words, when it comes from attention rather than avoidance. When it honors what the moment requires instead of rushing to define it.

That kind of presence takes time to learn. It forms in places where answers fall short. It's shaped by loss, by watching pain unfold without a fix, by staying close anyway.

By this stage of life, I've learned to recognize when someone is offering their full attention and when they're just waiting to speak. I can tell when a room tightens. I can feel when someone wants to be witnessed, not reassured.

Presence is more than stillness. It's a form of listening with the whole body.

And it's shaped, over time, into a practice that needs no announcement.

Sometimes that looks like holding your ground in a conversation that could easily slide into small talk. Sometimes it means keeping a boundary without offering a full explanation. Sometimes it's the simple act of returning, again, to a place where your presence helps steady the rhythm, even if no one says it out loud.

This kind of showing up doesn't come from duty. It comes from clarity.

Psychologist James Hillman once said that the soul doesn't need to be fixed, it needs to be accompanied. That holds true in spiritual presence, too. We don't need to interpret everything. We need to remain long enough for the meaning to surface.

I once read about a hospice nurse who described her work in simple terms. She stayed with the ones arriving to say goodbye. No guiding, no interpreting, just a steady nearness that allowed the moment to unfold. She let silence stand.

That kind of presence has come back to me more than once. Especially when I'm sitting across from someone whose grief has no words. When the only faithful response is to remain still. I've learned to trust that presence can speak what language cannot.

This isn't about solving. It's about staying calibrated.

You might never know what your presence allowed. You may never hear what shifted. You may offer years of consistency with no formal acknowledgment. The point isn't impact you can track. It's trust you can stand in.

And that trust forms something in you.

The more often you show up this way, the more your inner response changes. You speak less out of habit. You move with greater intention. You become more porous, not emotionally raw, but spiritually accessible.

Jesus lived this. He didn't flinch in uncomfortable rooms. He didn't rush to resolve what was still unfolding. He stayed with people, sitting, eating, asking questions, listening with patience that refused to hurry someone into clarity. His power wasn't separate from His presence. They came through the same door.

In Mark 5, when the woman reaches for His robe, He could have kept moving. But He stops. He waits. And in that pause, she speaks her full truth. Not a summary. Not a sanitized version. The whole story. That still moves me.

Because it reminds me what happens when presence makes room for wholeness.

This is the way I want to move now. No explanation required. Just an openness to the moment and whatever it might need from me, or not.

Some days that looks like staying through silence. Other times it means naming something others would rather avoid. Occasionally it means standing alone in a room full of surface-level chatter, refusing to shrink into it.

This practice rewires something deep.

Compassion grows thicker skin. Clarity softens. Patience starts to set the pace. You respond to disruption with less noise. You shift from proving to discerning.

And others notice. They mirror your energy. They pause before reacting. They follow your eyes instead of your volume.

This isn't performance. It's witness.

The discipline of presence includes rest. You learn how to exit without abandoning. You learn when silence is healing and when it's withholding. You let yourself regenerate before offering again.

I don't keep score anymore. I don't watch for results. I ask simpler questions: *Did I stay grounded? Did I stay open? Did I carry peace into a moment that didn't have it before?*

That's my measure now.

And on the days that leave me stretched, I return to the reason I began: Presence creates possibility. When I remain aligned, I don't need to predict the outcome. I just need to hold the space well.

This is the spiritual discipline of showing up.

Quiet. Consecrated. Clear.

It's how I live now.

Love as Legacy

I once thought legacy would come later, after the work, after the proving. A stretch of time when the pieces lined up and explained themselves. Something you could name, maybe even point to.

Love changed that.

Legacy turns out to be quieter. It shows up in how you speak to someone who's unsure. How you listen. How you hold space without needing to shape the outcome.

It shows up in how someone feels after they've spoken their truth. It lives in the pauses. In the restraint to listen fully before responding. In the way you carry steadiness when someone else falters. Love leaves a trace that doesn't require attention.

There are people I carry without naming. Their words still echo in mine. Their courage helped me move forward when mine was thin. Their grace made it easier to forgive. They didn't build monuments. They shaped memory.

That kind of legacy doesn't live in what we leave behind. It lives in what we pass forward.

Paul understood this. In his letter to the Corinthians, he wrote, *"If I have faith that can move mountains, but have not love, I am nothing... Love always protects, always trusts, always hopes, always perseveres. Love never fails."* (1 Corinthians 13:2, 7–8)

He wasn't offering a philosophy. He was describing a way of life.

Legacy takes root each time we choose love over fear. When we speak gently instead of stepping back. When we stay when leaving would be cleaner. When we bless even if no one's watching.

Some people write their names into history. Others write their love into people. The second kind carries farther.

This is the shape my offering takes now. I encourage where I see potential. I share what's been hard-won without needing credit. I pray for people who may never know. These choices aren't strategies. They're part of the rhythm.

Love doesn't need an audience. It needs sincerity.

Every day gives us the chance to begin again.

And love takes many shapes.

Sometimes it builds. Sometimes it releases. Sometimes it draws close. Sometimes it gives space. In each form, something essential takes hold.

That same rhythm of generativity still runs through this season. Erikson named it well, the shift that happens when we begin to care more about what we leave with others than what we keep for ourselves. It isn't about ambition. It's about release. A quiet knowing that experience becomes wisdom only when it's offered.

I notice it in small places. When I choose to wait instead of weigh in. When someone's story asks for space, and I let the silence hold it. A choice to offer what's been earned with no expectation in return. When a conversation calls for depth, I stay with it. When something weighty surfaces, I listen longer. I bring what I've gathered. I don't push it. I place it carefully where it might be useful.

Legacy isn't waiting for an ending. It's already moving through each choice that honors care over comparison, humility over credit, and presence over control.

The story we leave behind is formed by the kind of love we practice now.

I think often of those who shaped me without force. They didn't push. They didn't preach. They stayed aligned with who they were, and something in that clarity gave me permission to be more of who I am.

They didn't seek influence. They moved with intention, and something about that steadiness gave others permission to do the same. I found myself more grounded around them, less because of what they said, more because of how they were.

That kind of legacy doesn't draw attention to itself. It settles in. It lasts. It lasts in the way someone shows up without needing credit. In how they offer what they've earned, simply because they can.

I've seen love take shape in places that caught me off guard. A coworker echoing something I'd said weeks earlier. A patient softening during a moment of quiet. My husband's daughter responding with grace I once showed her. That's where the transmission happens. Without fanfare.

Love leaves its fingerprint in the small patterns.

In how we answer after a long day. In how we respond to regret. In how we extend compassion without asking for proof that it's deserved. Over time, these patterns form memory. Memory becomes meaning. Meaning becomes legacy.

The deepest part of this is rarely recognized. And that's what gives it strength.

Only a few people have left that kind of mark on me. A supervisor whose steadiness helped shape my own. A former lover who altered my rhythm in ways I still carry. A friend, older, radiant, whose presence reflects something unmistakably holy. And a colleague turned confidant who wasn't afraid to speak truth when I needed it most. None of them tried to be formative. They simply lived honestly, and something in that honesty moved me.

Each one carried something steady. Not because they were trying to make an impact, but because they moved through the world aligned with what mattered.

That kind of love stays with you.

Legacy begins right there.

Each conversation writes a line. Each generous moment plants a seed.

Each choice to act from wholeness rather than habit moves the story forward.

I no longer pursue legacy as something to earn. I let it grow from the days I live well. I trust the shape love takes as I offer it freely.

This kind of love blesses those who receive it, and those who give it. It reveals how much we've been entrusted with. It reminds us where we come from. It teaches us how God moves, quietly, consistently, through ordinary presence.

That's the legacy worth living.

Jesus framed it clearly: *"By this everyone will know that you are my disciples, if you love one another."* (John 13:35)

Jesus didn't highlight success. He named love as the marker.

That's where I take my cues now. I don't track what I've built. I pay attention to what I've made possible. Love that enters the room quietly and leaves it lighter. Love that steadies the air.

Where someone feels their shoulders drop. Where someone stops bracing.

Where someone begins to believe again that they are deeply known and wholly loved.

That's where legacy lives.

That's the ground I choose to walk.

Chapter Ten

THE FULLNESS OF TIME

Living With Mortality in View

I used to think of death as something that happened to other people.

That sounds naive, but it's the way most of us live for a long time. We carry death as a vague future event, a theoretical closing that floats somewhere at the end of a long line of good decisions. We know it's real. But we keep it in the distance. We plan. We save. We imagine ourselves decades from now, sitting in good chairs with good backs, telling stories to someone who wants to hear them.

But something shifts in the body around sixty. It's not a panic. It's not even fear, most days. It's a kind of reckoning. Your skin begins to say things your mouth hasn't. Your sleep changes. A new ache arrives in the same knee every morning. You find yourself forgetting what you were saying mid-sentence because your brain just let go of the thread. No alarm, just a quiet recognition: I have entered the final Act.

For me, it wasn't a single crisis moment. It was a series of small ones. I started reading obituaries more carefully. I noticed when someone just a few years older than me passed away "suddenly," as the notices always say. I began mentally mapping how much time I might have left, to live more intentionally. There was a season when I named my goals by what I hoped to build. Now I name them by what I hope to bless.

The difference matters.

Living with mortality in view doesn't mean giving up or winding down. It means living with full awareness of what's eternal, and what's not.

It means telling the truth, early and often. It means asking, *What am I still trying to prove, and why?* It means letting the young believe in progress while I begin to believe in presence. And presence doesn't require proof. It requires attention.

Scripture has always named this clearly, though we resist it. *"Teach us to number our days, that we may gain a heart of wisdom"* (Psalm 90:12). Not so we can fear death, but so we can live wisely inside its promise. Death, for the Christian, is not interruption. It is threshold. The shift from perishable to imperishable (1 Cor. 15:53). From dust to glory.

I don't claim to understand that fully. But I believe it.

Psychologically, there's a name for this stretch of life: "ego integrity versus despair," as Erik Erikson framed it. We either integrate the story of our lives, accept it, bless it, offer it, or we scramble. We try to outrun regret, to hoard meaning, to deny the body's slow fading. One leads to peace. The other leads to panic.

I've seen both. I've been both.

Some days, I'm deeply at peace with the shape my life has taken. Other days, I catch myself aching for a version that never came to pass. I hold pictures of who I meant to be. I mourn what I never became. Even that is holy ground.

The closer I move toward the end, the less I need a life that made sense to other people. I just want a life that was true.

So I speak more directly. I don't soften the truth to make it more palatable. I don't rehearse what I'm going to say. I just say it. I make moments with my husband just to be near him, not to solve anything, not to fill the space, but to show him I care, even when I have nothing profound to share. I spend less energy trying to impress anyone. I trust who I've become. I don't go looking for former versions of myself or thumb through old pages for meaning. I stay where I am. And I speak to God from here, present, honest, already seen.

Living with mortality in view means I no longer spend time in places where I can't bring my full self. It means I no longer buy into the culture's obsession with legacy-building. I believe in blessing, not branding. In a life lived forward, not a name preserved in stone.

We weren't made to be remembered by the masses. We were made to be remembered by the people we lived with. And loved.

I think of Jesus now not only in how He lived, but in how He ended. How He poured out. How He offered everything without spectacle. How He let Himself be broken. How He forgave before anyone asked. How He saw the thief beside Him and made room for one more in Paradise.

He didn't cling to His own glory. He emptied Himself (Philippians 2:7). And if I want to live like Him, then I have to be willing to end like Him, without clinging.

That's the work of this final stretch. No image to protect. No payoff to chase. Just the slow, deliberate work of laying things down. With clarity. With truth. With appreciation for what held, and acceptance of what didn't.

I don't know how many years I have left. But I know what kind of years I want them to be.

Attentive. Unhurried. Sharp-minded, soul-strong.

Rich in memory. Light in baggage.

Less proof. More presence. Less striving. More stillness. Less ladder. More light.

This is what mortality offers, not as a threat, but as a teacher. A final invitation to become what we always were: temporal, yes. But holy. Finite, but radiant with the breath of God.

If I treat these days as weighty, not because they're running out, but because they hold something holy, then I'll know I lived fully. I wasn't aiming for forever. I was aiming for faithful.

Completing the Story

There comes a point when the future no longer stretches out like a canvas. It narrows. Sharpens. It becomes less about what might still be built and more about what can be made whole.

That's the work of completion.

Completion doesn't mean finishing everything. It doesn't wrap life up like a novel with a clean last chapter. It means tending to what remains. Naming what was real. Giving shape to the story you've lived, even the parts that never landed where you hoped they would.

For years, I moved from one season to the next by instinct. Childhood to adulthood. Marriage to divorce. Faith to return. I adapted, pivoted, survived, healed. Completion asks something else. It asks you to turn around.

Reflection, yes, but more than memory. Completion is a gathering. A way of bringing your life back into your own hands. Not as résumé. As offering.

I think often of Paul, writing from prison: *"I have fought the good fight, I have finished the race, I have kept the faith"* (2 Timothy 4:7). He doesn't list his achievements. He names his endurance. His devotion. The language is lived, not measured.

What would it mean to say the same?

I stayed.

I remained faithful.

I offered what I had.

We've returned to Erik Erikson more than once, and with good reason. His framework has helped trace the shape of adulthood, the push to build, to belong, to bless. In this final stage, he names the choice between "integrity and despair." But by now, that conflict has evolved. It's no longer about how much we created or how well we performed. The question becomes: *What did we bless? What did we hold sacred? What truth do we carry now, and are we willing to place it in the hands of others?*

Photo albums still sit on a shelf, collecting dust. I haven't gone through the old boxes from my office. Or the ones still packed from a move over thirty years ago.

It isn't fear that keeps me from them. It's that I haven't needed to open them. Whatever's inside hasn't called for me. Completion, for now, looks like stillness. Letting the past sit where it is. One day I may want to take a stroll down memory lane, but that day hasn't arrived.

Still, I know the time will come. I'll need to sort through it eventually, but not for sentiment. For stewardship. Someone will open those boxes after I'm gone, and I'd rather do the choosing myself. What gets kept. What gets shredded. What no one else needs to carry. That, too, is part of leaving things whole.

I don't need photos or papers to understand the shape of my life. The coherence lives elsewhere, in the body, in the choices, in the tone of my voice when I speak from a place that no longer needs explaining. That's enough. That tells the truth.

This is where completion begins, not in clarity, but in the quiet honoring of what was lived. And the permission to let it rest.

It can be tempting to revise the story. To trim the edges, reframe the events, make the arc cleaner. But the sacred life doesn't require symmetry. It requires honesty. A life well-lived doesn't need resolution. It deepens through recognition.

Completion also asks us to release others.

Every parent knows the moment when a child chooses differently. Every friend eventually learns when presence matters more than counsel. Every long-held relationship, if it lasts, will ask you to yield something: the version you wanted, the last word, the memory you swore you'd keep as fact.

In this season, releasing others becomes an act of grace.

You begin to see you were never the author of anyone else's story. You were a companion. You stayed present. A steady hand at the edge of someone else's becoming.

That counts, too.

In Scripture, completion carries weight. God doesn't rush the process. He finishes what He begins, and when the work is done, He stops, not from fatigue, but because it's whole. *"Very good,"* He called it, before choosing rest (Genesis 2:2–3).

I've come to understand that kind of rest as its own kind of Sabbath. A pause that doesn't perform. A rhythm that makes room for gratitude instead of more effort.

Completion doesn't need a spotlight. It only needs to be recognized. For me, it looks like recognizing the years I pushed through without applause. It looks like sitting out on the deck on a lazy spring afternoon, breeze at my back, sun on my face, dog at my feet, listening to the birds, the squirrels, the frogs, sipping something warm and letting the day be enough. No performance. Just presence. Just life, quiet and unforced.

The soul doesn't tally. It gathers.

And God, in His mercy, doesn't grade our lives on resolution. He receives them. He knows every folded letter, every prayer whispered in the dark, every time we chose love over distance.

To complete the story is to say: I lived this. I gave what I had. I learned what I could. I hand it back, unpackaged, unpolished, open.

That is enough.

That is the fullness of time.

Trusting God With What Remains

There comes a moment, quiet, often unnoticed, when you realize the bulk of your decisions are behind you. The big moves have been made. You've chosen the path, however winding. You've built what you could, tended what you were given, offered what you had in your hands.

And still, life continues.

The question becomes: *What now?*

This stretch, often framed as a winding down, feels more like a laying bare. The roles that once held shape, parent, worker, partner, provider, begin to loosen. You start to see how much of your life has already been lived, and how much of the soul's work still remains.

There is always something left.

A part of the heart unoffered. A memory that hasn't settled. A conversation that waits for courage. A calling that never asked for a title, just time.

This is where trust deepens. Not because the answers multiply, but because stillness does.

As the rhythms shift, it becomes easier to hear God in the quiet. He rarely raises His voice. He asks simple questions in simple tones: *Will you trust me with this stretch? Will you trust me with what still lingers?*

It's easier to trust God when the outcome makes sense, when the effort leads somewhere, when something takes root. There's a kind of grounding in being able to say, "I helped bring that into the world."

But then there's everything that never took shape. The idea that stayed an idea. The door that never reopened. The silence that never broke. The part of you that was ready to offer something but never found the moment. And they still matter. They sit in the background, quiet and unfinished.

Even there, God doesn't turn away.

It takes a different kind of trust to hand Him those parts. The remnants. The threads that never tied together. You offer them without dressing them up. You say, "This is what's left. Do what You will."

Scripture tells this story again and again. A widow offers the last bit of flour (1 Kings 17). Five loaves and two fish feed thousands (Matthew 14). A mustard seed of faith moves mountains (Matthew 17:20). The pattern holds: God takes what others dismiss and calls it worthy. He multiplies what's offered. He sanctifies what remains.

This season calls for that kind of trust. Trust in His timing. Trust in His knowing. Trust that presence, in the end, is purpose enough.

Erikson shows up again here, and it makes sense. His final stage speaks of integrity: the ability to hold one's story without regret or revision. The theological echo is trust. A settled awareness that your story was always in God's hands, and still is.

Trust doesn't erase longing. I still long, for restoration, for resolution, for a few conversations that may never happen. But longing can be holy, too. It keeps the heart open. It pulls the soul forward.

God honors that kind of longing, the kind that turns toward Him, not away.

These days, my prayers are different. Shorter, but fuller. Less asking. More showing up. Sometimes I sit in silence and say, "You know." And He does. That's enough.

Trusting God with what remains means releasing the pressure to be noticed. Maybe your legacy has less to do with what you accomplished and more to do with how you carried things. How you showed up when it counted. How you kept your footing when others lost theirs. The quiet care you gave that no one asked for, but needed.

God doesn't miss any of it. Even when no one else saw them, He did. He carries it forward, whether or not we see the harvest.

In Luke's Gospel, Jesus tells a story about a fig tree that isn't producing. The landowner's ready to cut it down, but the gardener steps in. Give it one more year, he says. Let me tend to it a little longer, loosen the soil, give it what it needs. Then we'll see what grows. That's the kind of God I believe in, the One who tends the slow bloom. The One who sees promise where others see waste.

There is grace in trusting a gardener like that.

He knows what season you're in better than you do. He knows what can still grow. He receives whatever you offer, even if it feels late or small.

I no longer measure what remains.

Most mornings, I hand Him what's left, this body with its own limits, this mind with its patterns, this soul still looking for ways to be useful. Some days I feel it more than others. But He shows up the same either way. No pressure. No checklist. Just presence. Just stay.

These days, trust feels less like belief and more like proximity.

And the older I get, the less I ask God to fix anything. These days, I ask for less. Mostly that He stay near.

And somehow, He does. Without needing to be summoned.

That steadiness, that's what holds me now.

It doesn't need to be more.

Eternal Light, Present Grace

Some evenings, I watch the sun slip low across the sky. The light softens. The shadows stretch. The colors turn, orange, pink, deep red, like the sky is making peace with the day. I sit still and let it happen. No need to reflect. No need to record. Just presence. This is when I feel closest to God, not in some orchestrated quiet time, but in the honesty of light fading and the permission to do the same.

The older I get, the more I experience time as invitation rather than measurement. The calendar holds less weight. The to-do list no longer defines anything worth doing. What matters most comes quietly, kindness, truth spoken plainly, and breath (no, seriously, breathing is a thing).

This is the grace of later years: to see with eternal eyes what once demanded performance. To love without needing control. To meet the moment as it is, not as something to manage, but something to receive.

In Scripture, eternity isn't just about the hereafter. It's something already at hand. Jesus said the Kingdom is *"within you"* (Luke 17:21). He didn't offer escape. He offered presence. He didn't frame life as something deferred. He called people to wake up to it.

I used to think eternity would begin at the end. These days, I'm more convinced it already exists now, running alongside this life, wrapped around it somehow. Not visible, but close. I sense it in moments that land heavier than they should. A stretch of silence that feels inhabited. A sense of being accompanied, even with no one else in the room. A pause in the day when time seems to ease up, no urgency, no measurement, just presence. I can't explain it. I don't try to name it. But every now and then, something in me goes still, and I know I've brushed up against something outside the usual flow. If that isn't eternity, it's close enough to keep me paying attention.

The old hymns carried this mystery long before I could name it. "Blessed assurance, Jesus is mine." The line never asks for evidence, it names what's already known. Assurance, for me, doesn't come from having it all figured out. It comes from knowing I'm still held, even on the days when I don't feel steady. That kind of grace doesn't wait for things to resolve. It shows up in real time and makes room.

I've been through seasons that wore my faith thin, grief, disappointment, questions I stopped trying to answer. Some relationships never found their way back. Some longings never lifted. They just settled in and made room for other things. Even so, I'm here. Still upright. Still carried by something I didn't manufacture.

What gets my attention now is this: God doesn't step back. He stays close. Maybe not in ways that dazzle, but in ways that don't go dark. Like steady breath. Like warmth that doesn't leave, even when the fire burns low.

Ecclesiastes says God *"has made everything beautiful in its time. He has also set eternity in the human heart"* (Eccl. 3:11). That feels truer with age. The longing for forever doesn't fade, but neither does the grace of right now.

To live in both at once is to carry light without needing to shine.

Present grace has changed the way I move through the world. I say less, and it means more. I give space without retreating. I listen longer. I pray with fewer words. I no longer need to prove anything. I simply show up.

The eternal doesn't rush. It lingers. It waits.

That's the invitation now: to become a vessel of that light. To live as though eternity already lives in me. To respond with care. To bless without needing notice. To meet the moment and let it be enough.

The sacred doesn't always show up loud. Sometimes it's tucked into the ordinary. A quiet moment. A slow breath. A steady goodbye.

Even as things change, bodies, relationships, memory, something solid holds underneath it all. And as I think about the end of this life, I don't picture fear. I picture rest. A crossing into something I've already brushed against more than once.

I imagine God meeting me there. Not startled by my arrival. Just steady. Familiar. As if He's been waiting in a place I've passed by before.

Whatever eternity turns out to be, I don't expect it to feel foreign.

And grace? Grace has always known where I live.

And somehow, even there, something holy was forming under the surface.

Even false selves are built from sacred longing.

In those years, the hunger for love looked like effort. The search for safety looked like perfectionism. But through all the adapting, the real self remained. Waiting. Watching. Rooting quietly into the center of me.

Eventually, becoming gave way to something new. Not because the self was complete, but because it was time to live it.

The next stretch of life asked for embodiment. For steadiness. For staying. I built a family. Raised a daughter. Reentered school. Relearned what I was capable of. Found my way into IT, not quickly, not dramatically, but with fidelity. Through study, late nights, missed meals, borrowed strength.

There were losses. Detours. Changes I didn't choose. But I kept showing up. And what I learned, again and again, was that presence mattered more than progress.

In that middle movement, everything turned practical. I didn't need a promotion, I needed peace. Somewhere along the way, I stopped performing and started paying attention. The choices I made began to echo what I actually believed, and life, almost imperceptibly, began to steady itself around that truth. I stepped back from relationships that blurred my voice. I spoke plainly, even when it risked the quiet. I parented my daughter trusting that she belonged to God, that He gave her to me to shepherd but not keep. I found a cadence in work, in friendship, and in faith.

The grace of that season wasn't that it was easy. The grace was that I didn't have to pretend.

And slowly, I began to understand what it meant to belong. Not as performance. As presence. To belong to God. To my own body. To a life I was no longer trying to escape.

The third movement arrived quietly. No clear line. Just a loosening. A gentle unfastening of roles that no longer held weight.

The ladder disappeared. The map softened.

And what remained was offering.

Not a legacy in the usual sense. I don't need my name remembered. But I do want my life to bless.

That blessing doesn't arrive through effort. It comes through alignment. Through atmosphere. Through the quiet way others begin to feel steadier in your presence because you've done the work to be steady yourself.

This stretch is no longer about ambition. It's about availability.

I don't perform wisdom. I practice it. Sometimes in the way I listen. Sometimes in how I leave silence unfilled. Sometimes just by showing up where I said I'd be, and letting that be enough.

Everything I used to reach for has softened into release. I still carry purpose. But it no longer carries me.

I offer what I've been entrusted with. I speak when it feels honest. I rest when I need to rest. And in all of it, I trust God to do with my life what only He can do, make meaning from the moments I could never have orchestrated.

Each movement carried its own holy work:

Becoming revealed how early hunger shapes us, but does not define us.

Belonging taught me how to live without losing myself.

Blessing now invites me to offer what remains, open-handed, without control.

None of it was wasted.

The years I spent performing didn't go to waste. The long pauses that felt empty, they were still forming something in me. Even the mess, the parts I tried to hide or minimize, held their own kind of weight.

Silence taught me how to listen. Unraveling made space for something more honest to emerge.

What makes a life holy isn't that it avoids pain. It's that God keeps showing up inside it.

So wherever you find yourself, still in the ache of becoming, deep in the work of belonging, or beginning to offer what you've carried, now this:

You are right on time.

The thread has not broken.

And the soul, ever faithful, still knows the way.

REFERENCES

American Psychiatric Association. (2013). *Diagnostic and statistical manual of mental disorders* (5th ed.). https://doi.org/10.1176/appi.books.9780890425596

Bowlby, J. (1988). *A secure base: Parent-child attachment and healthy human development.* Basic Books.

Briere, J. N., & Scott, C. (2015). *Principles of trauma therapy: A guide to symptoms, evaluation, and treatment* (2nd ed.). SAGE Publications.

Brown, B. (2012). *Daring greatly: How the courage to be vulnerable transforms the way we live, love, parent, and lead.* Gotham Books.

Courtois, C. A., & Ford, J. D. (Eds.). (2013). *Treating complex traumatic stress disorders in adults: Scientific foundations and therapeutic models* (2nd ed.). The Guilford Press.

Ebaugh, H. R. F. (1988). *Becoming an ex: The process of role exit.* University of Chicago Press.

Erikson, E. H. (1950). *Childhood and society.* W. W. Norton & Company.

Erikson, E. H. (1982). *The life cycle completed.* W. W. Norton & Company.

Erikson, E. H. (1997). *The life cycle completed* (Extended version with Joan M. Erikson). W. W. Norton & Company.

Fosha, D., Siegel, D. J., & Solomon, M. (Eds.). (2009). *The healing power of emotion: Affective neuroscience, development & clinical practice.* W. W. Norton & Company.

Granqvist, P. (2002). *Attachment and religiosity in adolescence: A longitudinal study.* Journal of Research on Adolescence, 12(2), 245–261. https://doi.org/10.1111/1532-7795.00033

Hillman, J. (1996). *The soul's code: In search of character and calling.* Random House.

Jung, C. G. (1959). *Aion: Researches into the phenomenology of the self* (R. F. C. Hull, Trans.; 2nd ed.). Princeton University Press.

Jung, C. G. (1966). *Two essays on analytical psychology* (R. F. C. Hull, Trans.). Princeton University Press. (Original work published 1953)

Jung, C. G. (1969). *The structure and dynamics of the psyche* (Collected Works of C. G. Jung, Vol. 8, 2nd ed.). Princeton University Press.

Kegan, R. (1994). *In over our heads: The mental demands of modern life.* Harvard University Press.

Kohlberg, L. (1981). *The philosophy of moral development: Moral stages and the idea of justice* (Vol. 1). Harper & Row.

Maslow, A. H. (1971). *The farther reaches of human nature.* Viking Press.

Mezirow, J. (1991). *Transformative dimensions of adult learning.* Jossey-Bass.

Paul, A. M. (2014, October 1). *What is the science of 'adulting'?* The New York Times. https://www.nytimes.com/2014/10/05/magazine/what-is-the-science-of-adulting.html

Perel, E. (2017). *The state of affairs: Rethinking infidelity.* Harper.

Perry, B. D., & Szalavitz, M. (2006). *The boy who was raised as a dog: And other stories from a child psychiatrist's notebook.* Basic Books.

Rizzuto, A. M. (1979). *The birth of the living God: A psychoanalytic study.* University of Chicago Press.

Rogers, C. R. (1961). *On becoming a person: A therapist's view of psychotherapy.* Houghton Mifflin.

Schwartz, B. (2015). *Why we work.* Simon & Schuster.

Siegel, D. J. (2010). *The mindful therapist: A clinician's guide to mindsight and neural integration.* W. W. Norton & Company.

Siegel, D. J. (2012). *The developing mind: How relationships and the brain interact to shape who we are* (2nd ed.). The Guilford Press.

Spring, J. A. (2004). *How can I forgive you? The courage to forgive, the freedom not to.* HarperCollins.

van der Kolk, B. (2014). *The body keeps the score: Brain, mind, and body in the healing of trauma.* Viking.

The Holy Bible, English Standard Version. (2001). Crossway Bibles. John 15:2

The Holy Bible, King James Version. Proverbs 22:6, Matthew 28:20

The Holy Bible, New International Version. (2011). Biblica, Inc. Genesis 2:15, Exodus 18:17–18, Exodus 20:9–10, Proverbs 16:31, Proverbs 20:29, Isaiah 30:21, Matthew 5:37, Matthew 6:21, Matthew 22:37–39, Mark 1:38, Mark 6:46, Luke 16:10, John 15:11, Romans 12:2, Romans 12:6, Ephesians 5:21, Colossians 3:23, 2 Timothy 4:6, 1 John 4:19

Weil, S. (1973). *Gravity and grace* (E. Craufurd, Trans.). Routledge. (Original work published 1947)

Winnicott, D. W. (1965). *The maturational processes and the facilitating environment: Studies in the theory of emotional development.* International Universities Press.

If This Book Moved You, You may find something in these other works by Renae C. Linde:

Into the Void

A profound meditation on time, memory, and the mystery of death.

If Before the Curtain Falls explores the richness of life's final act, Into the Void asks what happens when time itself unravels. This book doesn't try to resolve grief, it seeks to sit honestly in the silence it leaves behind. A poetic, philosophical, and spiritual reflection on what it means to vanish from time.

When We Let Go

A cultural and personal reckoning with effort, identity, and generational collapse.

For those drawn to the parts of Before the Curtain Falls that grapple with responsibility, legacy, and what it means to mature in an age of extended adolescence, When We Let Go offers a fierce yet compassionate critique of emotional avoidance, entitlement, and the quiet costs of carrying what others won't.

Toxic No More

Practical tools for unlearning destructive relational patterns and reclaiming emotional clarity.

If you're doing the internal work of releasing old narratives and learning how to show up with intention, this book is your companion. Thoughtful exercises and deep emotional insight guide readers through the trenches of transformation.

NONE OF IT WAS WASTED

Looking back, I see it differently now. Life wasn't a line. It wasn't a climb. It didn't follow the arc of progress the world kept insisting on. What took shape instead was something more layered. A rhythm. A return. A sacred sequence.

Three movements.

Each one essential.

Each one echoing the last.

There was a time I thought Act One was just childhood. But it extended much further. The becoming lasted longer than I expected.

It began in the chaos, learning how to read a room before I knew how to read a sentence. I adapted quickly. I learned to track tone, anticipate mood, hold my breath until it felt safe to speak. No one taught me to think in systems, but I learned anyway. It was the only way to survive.

Those early years were about becoming without language for what I was becoming. I performed well, stayed small, solved problems before they erupted. It looked like strength. It was survival.

About the Author

Renae C. Linde writes at the intersection of story, soul, and society. Her work ranges from spiritual memoir to cultural critique, always tracing the questions that surface at life's thresholds. She draws from lived experience as much as from psychology, philosophy, and faith, crafting books that invite readers to reflect on resilience, meaning, and the quiet work of love.

She lives and writes in the American Midwest, where she collects questions, keeps watch for wonder, and tries to name the things most people only feel.

"The soul doesn't move in straight lines."

www.ingramcontent.com/pod-product-compliance
Lightning Source LLC
Chambersburg PA
CBHW030452100526
44580CB00006B/100/J